INTOXICATED
BY MY
ILLNESS

INTOXICATED BY MY ILLNESS

And Other Writings
on Life and Death

Anatole Broyard

Compiled and edited
by Alexandra Broyard

Foreword by Oliver Sacks, M.D.

CLARKSON POTTER / PUBLISHERS
NEW YORK

Permission gratefully received from *The New York Times* to reprint the following articles: "The Literature of Death, Part I," "The Literature of Death, Part II," "Domesticating Death," "Life Before Death," "Intoxicated by My Illness," "Toward a Literature of Illness," "Doctor Speak to Me." (These pieces have been edited slightly to avoid repetition.)

"The Patient Examines the Doctor" and "Toward a Literature of Illness" have been expanded with material from a talk given at the University of Chicago Medical School in April 1990 and from the author's notes and preliminary writings.

Published by Clarkson N. Potter, Inc., 201 East 50th Street, New York, New York, 10022. Member of the Crown Publishing Group.
CLARKSON N. POTTER, POTTER, and colophon are trademarks of Clarkson N. Potter, Inc.
Manufactured in the United States of America

Library of Congress Cataloging-in-Publication Data

Broyard, Anatole.
    Intoxicated by my illness: and other writings on life and
death. / Anatole Broyard. — st ed.
p. cm.
1. Broyard, Anatole—Health. 2. Critics—United States—
Biography. 3. Cancer—Patients—United States—Biography.
I. Title
PS29.B76A3 1992
362.1′9699463′092—dc20
[B]   91-43719   CIP

ISBN 0-517-58216-3
10 9 8 7 6 5 4 3 2 1
First Edition

It was the last nostalgia: that he
Should understand.

WALLACE STEVENS

"Esthétique du Mal"

We say that God and the imagination are one . . .
How high that highest candle lights the dark.

WALLACE STEVENS

Final Soliloquy of the
"Interior Paramour"

ACKNOWLEDGMENTS

My gratitude and heartfelt thanks to Evelyn Toynton, Bliss Broyard, and Michael Vincent Miller for their help with this book. Evelyn edited the talk that Anatole gave at the University of Chicago so that its tone would be in keeping with his written words. Bliss, our daughter, contributed her skills and energy at those times when the material was slow to take shape, and Michael guided me through the various stages of this project. Also, a very special thank-you to Carol Southern, the editor of this book, who fulfilled that function with attentiveness and generosity of time and spirit.

CONTENTS

Foreword   xi

Prologue   xvii

PART ONE: Intoxicated by My Illness   1

PART TWO: Toward a Literature of Illness   9

PART THREE: The Patient Examines the Doctor   31

PART FOUR: Journal Notes May–September,

1990   59

PART FIVE: The Literature of Death 1981–1982   69

PART SIX: What the Cystoscope Said   89

Epilogue   133

FOREWORD

Anatole Broyard always wrote with the full force of his intellect and personality—and there seemed to be nothing, nothing genuine, that did not excite his interest. The subjects of illness and death, however, held a very special place for him, partly perhaps because his father, to whom he was so attached, died slowly (and, so to speak, in great detail) from a cancer when Anatole himself was a young man. As his wife, Alexandra, observes in the epilogue to these collected writings, this experience, this deep knowledge of death, "gave shading and resonance to the rest of Anatole's life."

In 1954 he published an intensely personal and powerful narrative of his father's last illness and death, "What the Cystoscope Said," and twenty-seven years later, in 1981 and 1982, he wrote a series of essays on "The Literature of Death." Anatole Broyard had already faced death, then, as a son, and as a literary critic, had already shown himself to be on very intimate (but also pugnacious) terms with what all of us, sooner or later, have to face. But personally he always enjoyed robust health, and did so until 1989, when he was suddenly struck with cancer, cancer of the prostate (akin to the bladder cancer that killed his father).

Illness, clearly, did not deprive Broyard of his curiosity or force—it sharpened it, focused it, as never before. He felt energized, "intoxicated," by his illness, and determined to face it, to write about it, with all the strength he could. And in these last writings of his, when he was (and knew himself to be) mortally ill, he brings a force, a clarity, a wit, an urgency, an intense feeling for the metaphoric and poetic powers of illness, which make them the equal of anything that has been written on the subject, by writers from Tolstoy to Susan Sontag.

I have never seen any writing about illness that is more forthright—nothing is glossed over, or evaded, or sentimental-ized, or pietized—and that is at the same time deeper, more intelligent, more reflective and resonant. You feel the man himself—who is also and always a critic and an artist—seize his pen with unprecedented force, determined to challenge his illness, to go into the very jaws of death, fully alive, pen in hand, a reporter, an analyst, to the last. He takes his pen almost to the darkness. His final journal notes go to within a few days of his death.

Broyard quotes an episode from Mary-Lou Weisman's

book *Intensive Care* on how just before her fifteen-year-old son died of muscular dystrophy, he asked his father to arrange him in an "impudent position" in the hospital bed. "I'd like my writing to be impudent," Broyard writes; "the threat of dying ought to make people witty." And it does, at least with him. *Intoxicated by My Illness* is a marvelously impudent book—opinionated, idiosyncratic, provocative, unrepentant; Broyard is completely alive, completely himself, even when he is dying—his wit, his chutzpah, are with him to the last.

In "Toward a Literature of Illness," Broyard writes of how little we can bear the thought of an anonymous illness, how we need to make illnesses metaphorical, to make them our own, and how we need always to be ill, and to die, with *style.* And how people, if they become ill, must become story-tellers, must make a story, metaphors, of their illness.

My initial experience of illness was as a series of disconnected shocks, and my first instinct was to try to bring
it under control by turning it into a narrative. Always in
emergencies we invent narratives. . . . Storytelling seems
to be a natural reaction to illness. . . . Stories are antibodies against illness and pain. . . . In the beginning, I
invented mininarratives. Metaphor was one of my symptoms. I saw my illness as a visit to a disturbed country,
rather like contemporary China. I imagined it as a love
affair with a demented woman who demanded things I
had never done before.

First, then, Broyard found himself making a narrative for himself. And then, almost at once, for others too. In these writings, Broyard discovers a tremendous, unprecedented freedom in being ill, a freedom (perhaps for the first time in his life) to say exactly what he wants, and to be just as crazy as he wants.

A critical illness is like a great permission, an authorization or absolving. It's all right for a threatened man to be romantic, even crazy, if he feels like it. All your life you think you have to hold back your craziness, but when you're sick you can let it out in all its garish colors.

The final necessity is to *possess* one's illness, to make it one's own. "It seems to me," he writes, "that every seriously ill person needs to develop a style for his illness." Some of the finest writing in *Intoxicated by My Illness* is precisely about finding or making such a style. Broyard went into the darkness jauntily, with style; and even to read about this makes the rest of us feel death as less engulfing and anonymous and gray.

For me, as a physician, the most extraordinary part of an extraordinary book is the essay "The Patient Examines the Doctor." Broyard speaks—as Auden did, in his last poems—about the sort of doctor he wants to have, and to talk to, and to be with, when Fate has struck and his last days are upon him. He would least of all want a doctor who is *bland,* one who does not seem "intense and willful enough to prevail over something powerful and demonic like illness."

What he does want in a doctor is "one who is a close reader of illness and a good critic of medicine . . . who is not only a talented physician, but a bit of a metaphysician, too . . . [one who is] able to go beyond the science into the person . . . imagine the aloneness of the critically ill . . . I want him to be my Virgil, leading me through my purgatory or inferno, pointing out the sights as we go."

The British psychoanalyst D. W. Winnicott, Broyard tells us at the end of his last essay "Intoxicated by My Illness," began an autobiography that he never finished. It begins, "I died," and a few paragraphs later says, "Let me see. What was happening when I died? My prayer had been answered. I was alive when I died." This, Broyard tells us, is why he wants to write his book—to make sure he'll be alive when he dies. Broyard never completed an autobiography, but these marvelous last writings can, in all sorts of ways, serve as one. It is quite certain that, as for Winnicott, his prayer was answered; he was intensely alive to the moment of his death, he saw Death clearly, he battled him to the last. Reading such a book as this, one wants to say, "Death, where is thy sting? O Grave, where is thy victory?"

OLIVER SACKS, M.D.

PROLOGUE

The writings in this book arise from the desire to face illness and death and bring them into the fabric of life. My husband, Anatole Broyard, was diagnosed with metastatic prostate cancer in August 1989, and this sudden confrontation with mortality inspired him to write about his experience. He was well prepared to do this. When he was twenty-eight, his father died of cancer—an event that led him throughout his life to think about the questions raised by illness and dying.

For the past nineteen years Anatole had written reviews and articles for The New York Times. *He had been a daily book critic and, later, an editor of* The New York Times Book Review. *Writing and books had always been a part of his life. As a young man after World War II, he opened a bookstore on Cornelia Street in Greenwich*

Village. Lacking the patience to sit and talk to his customers, he turned to writing essays and stories that were published in literary magazines and anthologies. Free-lance advertising jobs helped to pay the rent. He also taught fiction writing at the New School for Social Research, Columbia University, and later at New York University and Fairfield University.

When Anatole learned that he was ill, he responded by talking and then by writing about his situation. Anatole was a superb storyteller, and at this most difficult time of his life he concentrated his talents in a way that enabled him to hope and believe that he could outwit his cancer by constructing an alternative narrative that would wither and erase the shadow of death.

He did not conquer his cancer, but he triumphed in the way he lived and wrote about it. In a talk he gave six months before he died he said, "Dying is the end of illness. It is the further shore of illness. There's a wonderful book called The Wilder Shores of Love. *Well, dying is the wilder shore of illness."*

This is a book from that "wilder shore."

ALEXANDRA BROYARD

PART ONE

INTOXICATED BY MY ILLNESS

So much of a writer's life consists of assumed suffering, rhetorical suffering, that I felt something like relief, even elation, when the doctor told me that I had cancer of the prostate. Suddenly there was in the air a rich sense of crisis—real crisis, yet one that also contained echoes of ideas like the crisis of language, the crisis of literature, or of personality. It seemed to me that my existence, whatever I thought, felt, or did, had taken on a kind of meter, as in poetry or in taxis.

When you learn that your life is threatened, you can turn toward this knowledge or away from it. I turned toward it. It was not a choice but an automatic shifting of gears, a tacit agreement between my body and my brain. I thought that time had tapped me on the shoulder, that I had been given a real deadline at last. It wasn't that I believed the cancer was going to kill me, even though it had spread beyond the prostate—it could probably be controlled, either by radiation or hormonal manipulation. No. What struck me was the startled awareness that one day something, whatever it might be, was going to interrupt my leisurely progress. It sounds trite, yet I can only say that I realized for the first time that I don't have forever.

Time was no longer innocuous, nothing was casual anymore. I understood that living itself had a deadline—like the book I had been working on. How sheepish I would feel if I couldn't finish it. I had promised it to myself and to my friends. Though I wouldn't say this out loud, I had promised it to the world. All writers privately think this way.

When my friends heard I had cancer, they found me surprisingly cheerful and talked about my courage. But it has nothing to do with courage, at least not for me. As far as I can tell, it's a question of desire. I'm filled with desire—to live, to write, to do everything. Desire itself is a kind of immortality. While I've always had trouble concentrating, I now feel as concentrated as a diamond or a microchip.

I remember a time in the 1950s when I tried to talk a friend of mine named Jules out of committing suicide. He had already made one attempt, and when I went to see him he said, "Give me a good reason to go on living." He was thirty years old.

I saw what I had to do. I started to sell life to him, like a real estate agent. Just look at the world, I said. How can you not be curious about it? The streets, the houses, the trees, the shops, the people, the movement, and the stillness. Look at the women, so appealing, each in her own way. Think of all the things you can do with them, the places you can go together. Think of books, paintings, music. Think of your friends.

While I was talking I wondered, Am I telling Jules the truth? He didn't think so, because he put his head in the oven a week later. As for me, I don't know whether I believed what I said or not, because I just went on behaving like everybody else. But I believe it now. When my wife made me a hamburger the other day I thought it was the most fabulous hamburger in the history of the world.

With this illness one of my recurrent dreams has finally come true. Several times in the past I've dreamed that I had committed a crime—or perhaps I was only accused of a crime, it's not clear. When brought to trial I refused to have a lawyer—I got up instead and made an impassioned speech in my own defense. This speech was so moving that I could feel myself tingling with it. It was inconceivable that the jury would not acquit me—only each time I woke before the verdict. Now cancer is the crime I may or may not have committed, and the eloquence of being alive, the fervor of the survivor, is my best defense.

The way my friends have rallied around me is wonderful. They remind me of a flock of birds rising from a body of water into the sunset. If that image seems a bit extravagant or tinged with satire, it's because I can't help thinking there's something comical about my friends' behavior—all these witty men suddenly saying pious, inspirational things.

They are not intoxicated as I am by my illness, but sobered. Since I refuse to, they've taken on the responsibility of being serious. They appear abashed or chagrined in their sobriety. Stripped of their playfulness these pals of mine seem plainer, homelier—even older. It's as if they had all gone bald overnight.

Yet one of the effects of their fussing over me is that I feel vivid, multicolored, sharply drawn. On the other hand— and this is ungrateful—I remain outside of their solicitude, their love and best wishes. I'm isolated from them by the grandiose conviction that I am the healthy person and they are the sick ones. Like an existential hero, I have been cured by the truth while they still suffer the nausea of the uninitiated.

I've had eight-inch needles thrust into my belly, where I could feel them tickling my metaphysics. I've worn Pampers. I've been licked by the flames, and my sense of self has been singed. Sartre was right: You have to live each moment as if you're prepared to die.

Now at last I understand the conditional nature of the human condition. Yet, unlike Kierkegaard and Sartre, I'm not interested in the irony of my position. Cancer cures you of irony. Perhaps my irony was all in my prostate. A dangerous illness fills you with adrenaline and makes you feel very smart. I can afford now, I said to myself, to draw conclusions. All those grand generalizations toward which I have been building for so many years are finally taking shape. As I look back at how I used to be, it seems to me that an intellectual is a person who thinks that the classical clichés don't apply to him, that he is immune to homely truths. I know better now. I see everything with a summarizing eye. Nature is a terrific editor.

In the first stages of my illness, I couldn't sleep, urinate, or defecate—the word *ordeal* comes to mind. Then, when my doctor changed all this and everything worked again, what a voluptuous pleasure it was! With a cry of joy I realized how marvelous it is simply to function. My body, which in the last decade or two had become a familiar, no-longer-thrilling old flame, was reborn as a brand-new infatuation. I realize of course that this elation I feel is just a phase, just a rush of consciousness, a splash of perspective, a hot flash of ontological alertness. But I'll take it, I'll use it. I'll use everything I can while I wait for the next phase. Illness is primarily a drama, and it should be possible to enjoy it as well as to suffer it. I see now why the Romantics were so fond of illness—the sick man sees everything as metaphor. In this phase I'm infatuated with my cancer. It stinks of revelation.

As I look ahead, I feel like a man who has awakened from a long afternoon nap to find the evening stretched out before me. I'm reminded of D'Annunzio, the Italian poet, who said to a duchess he had just met at a party in Paris, "Come, we will have a profound evening." Why not? I see the balance of my life—everything comes in images now—as a beautiful paisley shawl thrown over a grand piano.

Why a paisley shawl, precisely? Why a grand piano? I have no idea. That's the way the situation presents itself to me. I have to take my imagery along with my medicine.

PART TWO

TOWARD A LITERATURE OF ILLNESS

I was reading *The Transit of Venus,* Shirley Hazzard's most recent novel. Though I admired her other books, I'd always resisted this one. It struck me as too pure, somehow; too heroic; larger or finer than life, and therefore unreal. But now I read it with an almost indescribable pleasure. There were sentences that brought tears of gratification to my eyes and raised the hairs on the nape of my neck.

I was in Brigham Hospital in Brookline, Massachusetts, propped up in bed with an intravenous feeding tube in my arm and a catheter in my urethral canal because a cystoscopy had left me unable to pee. It was a double room and my roommate, a kind of thug who growled when he spoke because he had both a broken jaw and a drug habit, was spraying the air for the fourth or fifth time that day with a cloying deodorizer. He had a television set and a radio going at the same time.

The catheter hurt, and the diagnosis of my case was ambiguous. When I asked the oncologist the usual question—How much time have I got?—he hesitated before answering.

"I would say," he said, "that you have in the neighborhood of years."

I burrowed into the book. I was not escaping into it but identifying with it as fervently as I have ever identified with any novel. The life Shirley Hazzard described was the kind I wanted to live for the rest of my life, for my neighborhood of years. Her book was the prescription I needed and that no doctor could give me. I needed a dose of the sublime. From where I sat in my cranked-up bed, the sublime seemed to be all there was left.

I paused in my reading because I was out of shape and the beauty of the book had winded me. In my mind I composed a letter to Shirley Hazzard. After a brief description of my circumstances, I said, "You offered me an alternative. Art is our ace in the hole. I'm eating your book for lunch, and it's making me hungry."

I was afraid of finishing *The Transit of Venus*. It had become my neighborhood. I put it down and went for a walk around the ward, dragging the metal rack with the IV tube and the catheter bag. From the window of an empty room I looked down at the city, which was dotted with trees. How extraordinary the real world was! Shirley Hazzard was right.

When I got out of the hospital my first impulse was to write about my illness. While sick people need books like *The Transit of Venus* to remind them of the life beyond their illness, they also need a literature of their own. Misery loves company—if it's good company. And surprisingly enough, there isn't much good company in this rapidly proliferating field. A critical illness is one of our momentous experiences, yet I haven't seen a single nonfiction book that does it justice. Even in fiction there are only a handful of great books on the subject: Tolstoy's *The Death of Ivan Ilyich,* Thoman Mann's *The Magic Mountain,* most of Kafka, and Malcolm Lowry's *Under the Volcano.*

While Tolstoy was the grandfather, my favorites among these are Mann and Lowry. Kafka's illnesses are more existential than physical; they are like Kierkegaard's "sickness unto death." In *The Magic Mountain,* Mann wrote the grand definitive romance of illness, a portrait that, I would say, speaking as a connoisseur now, will never be equaled. His description of life itself showed how precarious it was: "a form-preserving instability, a fever of matter . . . the existence of the impossible-to-exist, of a half-sweet, half-painful balancing, or scarcely balancing, in this restricted and feverish process of decay and renewal, upon the point of existence."

Mann's hero Hans Castorp, who has only a little "moist spot" on one lung, has been sublimating his passion for Clavdia Chauchat, who is seriously ill, by reading biology books. When, encouraged by champagne, Castorp woos her, he vacillates between the language of physiology, of the doctor, and the language of the lover or poet. "Let me touch devotedly with my lips," he says, "the femoral artery that throbs in the front of your thigh and divides lower down into the two arteries of the tibia! . . . The body, love, death," he says, speaking to her in French, the only language they have in common, "these three are only one. For the body is sickness and voluptuousness, and it is this that causes death, yes, they are carnal both of them, love and death, and that is their terror and their great magic!" After their first and only night together, Chauchat gives Castorp an X ray of her tubercular lungs as a souvenir.

Like Mann, Malcolm Lowry uses the delirium of illness in *Under the Volcano,* where alcoholism is the consul's disease—one that will kill him indirectly. While I have little patience with drunks, I love the consul, because he makes drunkenness too seem like "a fever of matter," like a slip or glitch in our composition, a hopeless reaching for happiness. He is so inventive, so poetic, so tender about his alcoholism, he wastes himself in such grandiose gestures and experiences such incredible distortions without allowing them to break his heart, that I find the novel almost unbearably moving.

When I turned to nonfiction, to books by people who were or had been ill, I expected to find some echo of Castorp or the consul, but for the most part I was disappointed. Two of the better books were written by reporters: *Stay of Execution,* by Stewart Alsop, who was a political columnist, and *Hanging in There,* by Natalie Spingarn, a medical reporter. Their books remind me of the dispatches of war correspondents. While they describe in considerable detail the way cancer attacks and how the campaign against it works, they don't go much beyond this. They tell the reader a lot about the waking life of the cancer patient, but not much about his daydreams or fantasies, about how illness transfigures you.

Their books are objective, businesslike. You wouldn't know from them that inside every seriously ill person there's a Kafka character, a Castorp, or a consul, trying to get out. On the other hand there are books about illness that are too eloquent, that are full of chanting and dying falls, so pious that they sound as if they were written on tiptoe. To be ill is an odd mixture of pathos and bathos, comedy and terror, with intervals of surprise. To treat it too respectfully is to fall into the familiar, florid traps of the Romantic agony.

Peter Noll, a Swiss professor of law, goes even further in avoiding the emotional aspect of illness. All through *In the Face of Death,* his strange book about having cancer, he argues, almost legalistically, that he has the right to refuse treatments that would disfigure him and make him impotent. He says that he prefers death to a sexless life in which he would have to wear a bladder on his abdomen. Yet the tone of his book is stoical and philosophical, and he hardly seems the kind of man to rate his potency and his physical vanity above life itself. The discrepancy is so noticeable that one senses a deep, repressed anger—even a secret tragedy—between the lines.

Max Lerner certainly has Mann and Kafka in bed with him in *Wrestling with the Angel: A Memoir of Triumph over Illness.* Like an old campaigner, he welcomes the opportunity to examine, at point-blank range, the threatened human body and soul. His book is the best of the patient's accounts I've seen. My only reservation about it is that his memoir is perhaps too intellectual, not lyrical enough, too much about ideas and too little about the whatness, the sheer here and now, of illness. His thinking about his illness is a bit too professional. Ill or well, he's the same Max Lerner, better known, almost, than the cancer he writes about. He's so firmly rooted in the human condition that he is not possessed by his condition as a critically ill person. At his age he's hard to awe.

Norman Cousins is both a reporter and a reformer in his books about his own and other people's illnesses. He was one of the first to encourage the patient to develop strategies of his own, to provide for himself all the things the doctor didn't order. While he has been criticized for oversimplifying the issues—his insistence, for example, on the healing power of laughter—he has many shrewd things to say. He advises the patient to regard the diagnosis of critical illness not as a threat or a prophecy but as a challenge. He urges the sick person to take an active part in his treatment, to keep reminding his doctor whose life it is.

In *Head First: The Biology of Hope,* his latest book, Mr. Cousins seems very useful in his job as a sort of patients' advocate in the School of Medicine at the University of California at Los Angeles. But while his book is crammed with information and news of research, he is perhaps too fond of unexplained remissions. I like him because he is an evangelist of sorts—and every hospital ought to have one—yet his sense of humor is corny and his yea-saying may put off sophisticated people. For a former editor of the *Saturday Review,* he has surprisingly little to offer about the imaginative life of the sick.

Bernie Siegel, a doctor who says "call me Bernie," is a

sort of Donald Trump of critical illness. He sounds like a proprietor or landlord of mortality. The title of his book, *Love, Medicine & Miracles,* tells a lot about him. He believes in love and miracles as much as in medicine, and he has even more spontaneous remissions to report than Norman Cousins. Although he's a surgeon, he might sometimes be mistaken for a pop psychiatrist. Like Mr. Cousins, he is not a gifted writer, and this may cause his suggestions to sound cruder than they actually are. He, like the Simontons, asks his patients to practice "imaging," to think of their "good" cells attacking and overcoming their "bad" cells. Some of his analyses of patients' drawings strike me as recklessly confident.

Yet, for better or worse, he introduces an element of camaraderie into the medical process. He rallies the patient and offers him hope, even if it is "inspirational." In his presentation of himself he reminds me of a doctor I knew who wore such outlandish-looking suits that I couldn't help wondering about his medical judgment. While his book is a best-seller, Dr. Siegel is like an awkwardly drawn angel announcing a controversial miracle. Yet, with all these caveats, he is a godsend to many people who are too sick to stick at his style.

For me, the trouble with most inspirational books is that you can feel them trying to inspire you. They're more "inspiring" than believable; you don't feel that you can trust them. I don't trust anyone who tells me that he loves me when he doesn't even know me. I think that a healthy critical attitude toward such literature is more "positive" than a half-hearted, rearguard attempt at saintliness or *agape.* Though I don't believe I can love my cancer away, I do think I may be able to shrink it a little by pointing out its limitations, by being critical of the way people bow down to it. I can treat it like an overrated text.

Susan Sontag's *Illness as Metaphor* and *AIDS and Its Metaphors* are elegant analyses of how we think about illness and the stigma we attach to it—the "spoiled identity" of the sick, as Erving Goffman puts it. She chooses to address herself more to the conceptualization of illness than to the daily experience of it. Approaching him panoramically rather than individually, she aims a bit high for the sick man lying flat in his hospital bed. It is not his quiddity but his place in the medical polity that occupies her. She is to illness what William Empson's *Seven Types of Ambiguity* is to literature.

In my opinion she's too hard on metaphor when she says that "the most truthful way of regarding illness—and the healthiest way of being ill—is one most purified of, most resistant to, metaphoric thinking." She seems to throw the baby out with the bath. While she is concerned only with negative metaphors, there are positive metaphors of illness, too, a kind of literary aspirin. In fact, metaphors may be as necessary to illness as they are to literature, as comforting to the patient as his own bathrobe and slippers. At the very least, they are a relief from medical terminology. If laughter has healing power, so, too, may metaphor. Perhaps only metaphor can express the bafflement, the panic combined with beatitude, of the threatened person. Surely Ms. Sontag wouldn't wish to condemn the sick to Hemingway sentences.

Oliver Sacks, a neurologist, has become a kind of poet laureate of contemporary medicine. While I can only hint here at all the extraordinary things he has done to open up our thinking about illness in *Awakenings, Migraine, A Leg to Stand On, The Man Who Mistook His Wife for a Hat,* and *Seeing Voices,* I would describe him as a doctor who has a genius for looking around inside the patient's illness for suggestions about how the sick man can cope, how he can live parallel to, or even through, his disability. He reconciles afflicted people to their environment in such a way that they are not so much submitting to it in an impaired exchange as proposing a novel relation. He turns disadvantages to advantage.

When Dr. Sacks severely injured his leg while climbing alone in Norway, he could hardly move and might easily have died of exposure, but as he says, "There came to my aid now melody, rhythm and music. . . . Now, so to speak, I was *musicked* along. I did not contrive this. It happened to me." An imaginative athlete of medical innovation, he finds more means of healing than are dreamed of in our philosophies.

I'm not a doctor, and even as a patient I'm a mere beginner. Yet I *am* a critic, and being critically ill, I thought I might accept the pun and turn it on my condition. My initial experience of illness was as a series of disconnected shocks, and my first instinct was to try to bring it under control by turning it into a narrative. Always in emergencies we invent narratives. We describe what is happening, as if to confine the catastrophe. When people heard that I was ill, they inundated me with stories of their own illnesses, as well as the cases of friends. Storytelling seems to be a natural reaction to illness. People bleed stories, and I've become a blood bank of them.

The patient has to start by treating his illness not as a disaster, an occasion for depression or panic, but as a narrative, a story. Stories are antibodies against illness and pain. When various doctors shoved scopes up my urethral canal, I found that it helped a lot when they gave me a narrative of what they were doing. Their talking translated or humanized the procedure. It prepared, strengthened, and somehow consoled me. Anything is better than an awful silent suffering.

I sometimes think that silence can kill you, like that terrible scene at the end of Kafka's *The Trial* when Joseph K. dies speechlessly, "like a dog." In "The Metamorphosis," a story that is now lodged in everybody's unconscious, Gregor Samsa dies like an insect. To die is to be no longer human, to be dehumanized—and I think that language, speech, stories, or narratives are the most effective ways to keep our humanity alive. To remain silent is literally to close down the shop of one's humanity.

One of my friends had lung cancer, and during an exploratory operation he suffered a stroke that left him speechless. For a month he lay in his hospital bed trying to talk to me and his other friends with his eyes. He was too depressed or too traumatized to write on a pad. He died not of cancer exactly, but of pneumonia, as if his lungs had filled with trapped speech and he had drowned in it.

Just as a novelist turns his anxiety into a story in order

to be able to control it to a degree, so a sick person can make a story, a narrative, out of his illness as a way of trying to detoxify it. In the beginning I invented mininarratives. Metaphor was one of my symptoms. I saw my illness as a visit to a disturbed country, rather like contemporary China. I imagined it as a love affair with a demented woman who demanded things I had never done before. I thought of it as a lecture I was about to give to an immense audience on a subject that had not been specified. Having cancer was like moving from a cozy old Dickensian house crammed with antiques, deep sofas, snug corners, and fireplaces to a brand-new one that was all windows, skylights, and tubular furniture.

Making narratives like this rescues me from the unknown, from what Ernest Becker called "the panic inherent in creation" or "the suction of infinity." If I were to demystify or deconstruct my cancer, I might find that there is no absolute diagnosis, no single agreed-upon text, but only the interpretation each doctor and each patient makes. Thinking about difficult situations is what writers do best. Poetry, for example, might be defined as language writing itself out of a difficult situation.

Like anyone who has had an extraordinary experience, I wanted to describe it. This seems to be a normal reflex, especially for a writer. I felt a bit like Eliot's Prufrock, who says, "I am Lazarus, come from the dead, / Come back to tell you all, I shall tell you all." Like a convert who's had a vision, I wanted to preach it, to tell people what a serious illness is like, the unprecedented ideas and fantasies it puts into your head, the unexpected qualms and quirks it introduces into your body. For a seriously sick person, opening up your consciousness to others is like the bleeding doctors used to recommend to reduce the pressure.

What goes through your mind when you're lying, full of nuclear dye, under a huge machine that scans all your bones for evidence of treason? There's a horror-movie appeal to this machine: Beneath it you become the Frankenstein monster exposed to the electric storm. How do you appear to yourself when you sit with bare shins and no underwear beneath a scanty cotton gown in a hospital waiting room? Nobody, not even a lover, waits as intensely as a critically ill patient. On a more complicated level, it would be like explicating a difficult poem to try to capture the uncanny, painless yet excruciating sensation that comes with having a needle thrust straight into your abdomen, a needle that seems to be writing on your entrails, scratching some message you can't make out.

When my father died, I tried to write a novel about it, but I found that my whole novel was written politely. I was so pious about death that it was intolerable, and I find that people are doing that to me now. They're treating me with such circumspection. They're being so nice to me. I don't know whether they really mean what they say or whether they're accommodating me. It's as though they're talking to a child, and I want them to stop that. I can't find them anymore. I need their help, but not in this form. The therapist Erving

Polster defined embarrassment as a radiance that doesn't know what to do with itself. We need a book that will teach the sick man's family and friends, the people who love him, what to do with that radiance. If they knew how to use it, their radiance might do him more good than radiation.

The space between life and death is the parade ground of Romanticism. The threat of illness itself seems to sound a Romantic note—I've been feeling exalted since I heard the diagnosis. A critical illness is like a great permission, an authorization or absolving. It's all right for a threatened man to be romantic, even crazy, if he feels like it. All your life you think you have to hold back your craziness, but when you're sick you can let it out in all its garish colors.

I'm reminded of an experiment described by Joan Halifax and Stanislav Brof in a book called *The Human Encounter with Death*. Working in a hospital with terminally ill people, they noticed that many of them were so depressed, either by their illness or by the thought of dying, that they couldn't, or wouldn't, talk to the friends and relatives who came to see them. Some of them wouldn't even talk to themselves. In an attempt to relieve their depression, these two psychologists gave certain patients controlled doses of hallucinogens. While this didn't work for everyone, in some cases it produced a blaze of revelation that must have been a final or terminal joy for the patient, his family, and his friends. I would like my writing to have some of this blaze if I can fan it.

Writing is a counterpoint to my illness. It forces the

cancer to go through my character before it can get to me. In *Intensive Care,* Mary-Lou Weisman tells us that just before her fifteen-year-old son died of muscular dystrophy, he asked his father to arrange him in an "impudent position" in the hospital bed. I'd like my writing to be impudent. While Norman Cousins looks for healing laughter in low comedy, I'd rather try to find it in wit. The threat of dying ought to make people witty, since they are already concentrated. Oddly enough, death fits Freud's economic definition of wit: He says that we set aside a certain amount of energy to hear out a joke that threatens to go on and on like life, and then suddenly the punch line cuts across it, freeing all that energy for a rush of pleasure.

Norman Cousins and Bernie Siegel are correct in saying that a sick person needs other strategies besides medical ones to help him cope with his illness, and I think it might be useful to describe some of the strategies that have occurred to me. After all, a critic is a kind of doctor of strategies. For example, I saw on television an Afro-Cuban band playing in the streets of Spanish Harlem. It was a very good band, and before long a man stepped out of the crowd and began dancing. He was very good, too, even though he had only one leg and was dancing on crutches. He danced on those crutches as other people dance on ice skates, and I think that there's probably a "dance" for every condition. As Kenneth Burke, one of our best literary critics, said, the symbolic act is the dancing of an attitude.

As a preparation for writing, as a first step toward evolving a strategy for my illness, I've begun to take tap-dancing lessons, something I've always wanted to do. One of my favorite examples of a patient's strategy comes from a man I know who also has prostate cancer: Instead of imagining his good cells attacking his bad cells, he goes to Europe from time to time and imposes Continental images on his bad cells. He reminds me that in an earlier, more holistic age, doctors used to advise sick people to go abroad for their health.

The illness genre ought to have a literary critic—in addition to or in reply to Susan Sontag—to talk about the therapeutic value of style, for it seems to me that every seriously ill person needs to develop a style for his illness. I think that only by insisting on your style can you keep from falling out of love with yourself as the illness attempts to diminish or disfigure you. Sometimes your vanity is the only thing that's keeping you alive, and your style is the instrument of your vanity. It may not be dying we fear so much, but the diminished self.

Somebody other than a doctor ought to write about the relation between prostate cancer and sexuality. As I understand it, the prostate gland is like a raging bull in the body, snorting and spreading the disease. All of the various treatments are designed to tame the prostate. There's room for hermeneutics here. Is desire itself carcinogenic?

It's not unnatural for the patient to think that it's sex that is killing him and to go back over his amatory history for clues. And of course this is splendid material for speculation, both lyrical and ironical. My first reaction to having cancer was lyrical—irony comes later. It's part of the treatment. While I don't know whether this is lyrical, ironical, or both, I'm tempted to single out particular women and particular practices that strike me now as more likely to be carcinogenic than others. Coitus interruptus, which was widely practiced before the Pill, seems a likely suspect, and oral sex comes to mind as putting a greater strain on the prostate. But after saying this, I want to make it clear that I certainly don't hold my cancer against these women—whatever I did, it was worth it. I have no complaints in that direction. I wouldn't change a thing, even if I had known what was coming. And though this is only a fantasy, this talk of femmes fatales and pleasure you can die of, it's part of the picture of the cancer patient, and I don't want to edit out anything that belongs to my case.

My urologist, who is quite famous, wanted to cut off my testicles, but I felt that this would be losing the battle right at the beginning. Speaking as a surgeon, he said that it was the surest, quickest, neatest solution. Too neat, I said, picturing myself with no balls. I knew that such a solution would depress me, and I was sure that depression is bad medicine. The treatment I chose—it's important to exercise choice, to feel that you have some say—is called hormonal manipulation. It blocks or neutralizes the prostate. It doesn't cure the cancer, but holds it at bay until a better treatment comes along.

The doctor warned me that, like radiation, hormonal manipulation would "kill my libido." I find this hard to believe, especially in the case of a writer, for whom sexuality is inseparable from consciousness. After three months of treatment this has not yet happened, and I persist in believing that it won't. I've been manipulating my sexual hormones all my life, and I don't see how a drug can deprive me of this privilege. My libido is lodged not only in my prostate, but in my imagination, my memory, my conception of myself, my appreciation of women and of life itself. It belongs as much to my identity and my aesthetics as it does to physiology. When the cancer threatened my sexuality, my mind became immediately erect.

If in the future the treatment should interfere with the mechanics of sex, I can imagine all kinds of alternate approaches. As John Dewey said, "We never know what we might find until we're forced to look." When I think about my childhood, it's clear to me that preadolescent children often have wonderful sexual experiences. There were games of Spin the Bottle that I'll never forget. I find now that I have terrific dreams about sex, and I wonder whether this kind of unconscious experience can be made available when I'm awake.

I've never thought that good sex was primarily a question of mechanics. Of course the mechanics help, but who knows what we might invent if we didn't rely on them so much? Couldn't there be another level of sexuality? Can the imagination, for example, have orgasms? Is it possible to discover an alternative mode—as signing is an alternative to speech—a form we haven't thought of yet, an avant-garde, nonobjective, postmodern sexuality? What would Oliver

Sacks say? I never understood, in *The Sun Also Rises,* why the castrated Jake Barnes and Lady Brett couldn't think of anything to do, why all that wanting had to go begging. In my own case, after a brush with death, I feel that just to be alive is a permanent orgasm.

Looking back over my history as an adult, I can remember how beautiful it was to think about sex, to anticipate it. Before sleeping with a woman I genuinely desired, I used to feel something like a religious meditation, one that was moving toward a miraculous vision. Yet when I read about sex now, it seems to me that we've surrendered too much of that vision to the pursuit of orgasm. Maybe such a vision is the better part of our sexuality. At least we don't lose the capacity for it with illness or age—if anything, the vision intensifies. On the other hand, we all know, even after "good" sex, that sense of anticlimax, a kind of amnesiac feeling of having lost sight of what we had been looking for.

A friend of mine has made thirty or forty million dollars finding lost or unrecognized masterpieces by great painters. When I asked him how he knew the painting in question was by Goya or Tintoretto, he said, "It's a sensual thing. I can feel it in my balls." If he can feel great paintings in his balls, I ask myself, why shouldn't I feel great sex in my sensibility? Of course I don't mean these speculations of mine to be taken altogether seriously—I'm simply free-associating to sex and sickness—but neither should cancer be taken with such deadly seriousness. I think there's much to be learned in speculating about it, just as medical researchers speculate and free-associate about cancer in laboratories. My laboratory is literature, and cures have been found here, too, for all kinds of ills.

There's too much talk about anger among the sick, and in the books about them, and I think they should be cautioned against this. The feeling of being unjustly singled out is a cancerous kind of thinking and you can't get rid of it in Elisabeth Kübler-Ross's screaming room. I'm sixty-nine years old, and I've never been seriously ill in my life—what have I got to be angry about? I think sick people are more frustrated by their illness than angry and that they should think about ways to go on with their lives as much as possible, rather than proclaiming their anger like King Lear on the heath. If you reflect that you probably helped to bring your illness on yourself by self-indulgence or by living intensely, then the illness becomes yours, you own up to it, instead of blaming something vague and unsatisfactory like fate. Anger is too monolithic for such a delicate situation. It's like a catheter inserted in your soul, draining your spirit.

Just before he died, Tolstoy said, "I don't understand what I'm supposed to do." Very sick people feel this kind of confusion, too, but I'd like to point out that there's a lot they can do. I feel very busy now, very usefully occupied. There are many ways a sick person can divert and defend, maybe even transcend, himself.

The British psychoanalyst D. W. Winnicott began an autobiography that he never finished. The first paragraph simply says, "I died." In the fifth paragraph he writes, "Let me see. What was happening when I died? My prayer had been answered. I was alive when I died. That was all I had asked and I had got it." Though he never finished his book, he gave the best reason in the world for writing one, and that's why I want to write mine—to make sure I'll be alive when I die.

PART THREE

THE PATIENT
EXAMINES
THE DOCTOR

I WANT TO BEGIN by confessing that I'm an impostor. I have had almost no relationship with doctors. Although I'm sixty-nine years old, I've only been sick once before in my life. I had a mysterious illness with a fever of 107 degrees, the highest fever ever recorded for a surviving adult in St. Vincent's Hospital, where Dylan Thomas died. I had a very curious relationship with the doctors. They came in groups of six. They seemed to be attached to each other like Siamese sextuplets. They looked at me. They shook their heads, and they left me lying in a pool of sweat. I was never diagnosed.

At that time, I was giving poetry lessons to an insane millionaire who had endowed a room at another hospital. I had myself moved to that hospital, where I had a refrigerator, push buttons, visits from women, and I recovered. So I know very little about the doctor-patient relationship, but I'm going to project an ideal, a foolish doctor-patient relationship, the sort of thing that, say, Madame Bovary expected from Rodolphe—a love affair with a doctor.

When in the summer of 1989 I moved from Connecticut to Cambridge, Massachusetts, I found that I couldn't urinate.

I was like Portnoy, in *Portnoy's Complaint,* who couldn't fornicate in Israel. I had always wanted to live in Cambridge and I was almost persuaded that I couldn't urinate because I was surprised by joy, in C. S. Lewis's phrase. Like Israel for Portnoy, Cambridge was a transcendent place for me.

When my inhibition persisted, I began to think about a doctor, and I set about finding one in the superstitious manner most people fall back on in this situation. I asked a couple I knew for a recommendation. To be recommended gives a doctor an aura, a history, a shred of magic. I thought of my disorder as a simple case—prostatitis is common in men of my age—but I still wanted a potent doctor.

I applied to this particular couple for a recommendation because they are the two most critical people I know: critics of philosophy, politics, history, literature, drama, and music. They are the sort of people for whom information is a religion. They hold Ph.D.'s in at least two fields, and the rigor of their conversation is legendary. To talk with them is an ordeal, a fatigue of fine distinctions, and I wanted a doctor who had survived such a scrutiny. I, too, believe in the magic of criticism.

They could only give me the name of their internist: They didn't know a urologist. Though they are older than I am, the austerity of their lives seems to have protected them from urological complaints. I called their physician, and he referred me to a urologist. The recommendation was diluted, but it was better than none and I made an appointment to see this urologist in a local hospital.

The visit began well. The secretary was attractive, efficient, and alert. She remembered my name. I was shown into a pleasant office and told that the doctor would be with me in a few minutes.

While I waited I subjected the doctor to a preliminary semiotic scrutiny. Sitting in his office, I read his signs. The diplomas I took for granted: What interested me was the fact that the room was furnished with taste. There were well-made, well-filled bookcases, an antique desk and chairs, a reasonable Oriental rug on the floor. A window opened one entire wall of the office to the panorama of Boston, and this suggested status, an earned respect. I imagined the doctor taking the long view out of his window.

On the walls and desk were pictures of three healthy-looking, conspicuously happy children, photographed in a prosperous outdoor setting of lawn, flowers, and trees. As I remember, one of the photographs showed a sailboat. From the evidence, their father knew how to live—and, by extension, how to look after the lives of others. His magic seemed good.

Soon the doctor came in and introduced himself. Let's go into my office, he said, and I realized that I had been waiting in the office of someone else. I felt that I had been tricked. Having already warmed to the first doctor, I was obliged to follow this second man, this impostor, into another office, which turned out to be modern and anonymous. There were no antiques, no Oriental rug, and no pictures that I could see.

From the beginning I had a negative feeling about this

doctor. He was such an innocuous-looking man that he didn't seem intense enough or willful enough to prevail over something powerful and demonic like illness. He was bland, hearty, and vague, polite where politeness was irrelevant. I felt that he would be polite even to my illness, whatever it might be. He reminded me of a salesman, with nothing to sell but his inoffensiveness. I didn't like the way he spoke: It struck me as deliberately deliberate, the speech of a man fixed in a pose, playing doctor. There was no sign of a tragic sense of life in him that I could see, no furious desire to oppose himself to fate. I realized, of course, that what I was looking for was unreasonable, that I was demanding nothing less than an ideal doctor. I sat there in this poor man's office and compared him to a heroic model I had summarily imagined.

In the end it didn't matter whether my reading of this particular doctor was just or unjust—I simply couldn't warm up to him. Choosing a doctor is difficult because it is our first explicit confrontation of our illness. "How good is this man?" is simply the reverse of "How bad am I?" To be sick brings out all our prejudices and primitive feelings. Like fear or love, it makes us a little crazy. Yet the craziness of the patient is part of his condition.

I was also aware of a certain predisposition in myself in favor of Jewish doctors. I thought of them as the troubleshooters—the physicians, lawyers, brokers, arbiters, and artists—of contemporary life. History had convinced them that life was a disease. My father, who was an old-fashioned Southern anti-Semite, insisted on a Jewish doctor when he developed cancer of the bladder. A Jewish doctor, he believed, had been bred to medicine. In my father's biblical conception, a Jew's life was a story of study, repair, and reform. A Jewish doctor knew what survival was worth because he had had to fight for his. Obliged to treat life as a business rather than a pleasure, Jews drove hard bargains. To lose a patient was bad business. In his heart I think my father believed that a Jewish doctor was closer to God and could use that connection to "Jew down" death.

This other, all-too-human doctor took me into an examining room and felt my prostate. It appeared to me that he had not yet overcome his self-consciousness about this procedure. Back in his office, he summed up his findings. There were hard lumps in my prostate, he said, which suggested tumors, and these "mandated" further investigation. He used the word "mandated" twice in his summary, as well as the word "significantly."

You don't really know that you're ill until the doctor tells you so. When he tells you you're ill, this is not the same as giving you permission to be ill. You eke out your illness. You'll always be an amateur in your illness. Only you will love it. The knowledge that you're ill is one of the momentous experiences in life. You expect that you're going to go on forever, that you're immortal. Freud said that every man is convinced of his own immortality. I certainly was. I had dawdled through life up to that point, and when the doctor told me I was ill it was like an immense electric shock. I felt galvanized. I was a new person. All of my old trivial selves fell away, and I was reduced to essence. I began to look around me with new eyes, and the first thing I looked at was my doctor.

I had no reason to believe that he was not good. He was in a good hospital. He was one of the major urologists there, and yet I continued to observe him with something like displeasure. He proposed to do a cystoscopy on me. He said he wanted to examine the architecture of my bladder. I pondered the word "architecture." Was it justified, or was he being pretentious? Was he trying to accommodate himself to my vocabulary by talking about the architecture of the bladder as though it had a vault like a cathedral, a timbered vault, a fan vault? I thought, I can't die with this man. He wouldn't understand what I was saying. I'm going to say something brilliant when I die.

But he was the only urologist I knew in Cambridge, and so, a few days later, I allowed him to perform a cystoscopy on me, a procedure in which a small scope was inserted through my urethra up to my prostate and bladder. During surgical procedures, doctors wear a tight-fitting white cap, a sort of skullcap like the one Alan Alda wears on *M*A*S*H*. To this my doctor had added what looked like a clear plastic shower cap, and the moment I saw him in these two caps, I turned irrevocably against him. He wore them absolutely without inflection or style, with none of the jauntiness that usually comes with long practice. Now, I think a doctor who has been around, he knows how to do these things. There was no attempt to mitigate the two caps. The first was like a condom stuck on his head. He didn't look good in it. He had a round face, and in the cap he looked confused and uncertain. He wore it like an American in France who affects a beret without understanding how to shape or cock it. To my eyes this doctor simply didn't have the charisma to overcome or assimilate those caps, and this completed my disaffection.

I want to point out that this man was in all likelihood an able, even a talented, doctor. Certainly I'm no judge of his medical competence, nor do I mean to criticize it. What turned me against him was what I saw as a lack of style or magic. I realized that I wanted my doctor to have magic as well as medical ability. It was like having a *lucky* doctor. I've described all this—a patient's madness—to show how irrational such transactions are, how far removed from any notion of dispassionate objectivity. To be sick is already to be disordered in your mind as well. Still, this does not necessarily mean that I was wrong to want to change doctors: I was simply listening to my unconscious telling me what I needed. I feel that my absurdity is part of myself. I have to accommodate it. I wanted a doctor who would answer to my absurdity and triumph over it.

I think that if a man should ever give in to his prejudices, it's when he's ill. I used to teach a kind of literary sociology at the New School for Social Research in New York, and I used to say to my students, "For God's sake, cling to your prejudices. They're the only tastes you've got." I don't mean racial prejudices. I mean all prejudices, instinctive likes and dislikes. I'm convinced that my prejudice in the matter of medicine reflects the intelligence of my unconscious, and so I go with it. I need my prejudices. They're going to save me.

Now that I know I have cancer of the prostate, the lymph nodes, and part of my skeleton, what *do* I want in a doctor? I would say that I want one who is a close reader of illness and a good critic of medicine. I cling to my belief in criticism, which is the chief discipline of my own life. I secretly believe that criticism can wither cancer. Also, I would like a doctor who is not only a talented physician, but a bit of a metaphysician, too. Someone who can treat body and soul. There's a physical self who's ill, and there's a metaphysical self who's ill. When you die, your philosophy dies along with you. So I want a metaphysical man to keep me company. To get to my body, my doctor has to get to my character. He has to go through my soul. He doesn't only have to go through my anus. That's the back door to my personality.

I would hope that my doctor's authority and his charisma might help to protect me against what the anthropologist Richard Shweder calls "soul loss," a sense of terrible emptiness, a feeling that your soul has abandoned your ailing body like rats deserting a sinking ship. When your soul leaves, the illness rushes in. I used to get restless when people talked about soul, but now I know better. Soul is the part of you that you summon up in emergencies. As Mr. Shweder points out, you don't need to be religious to believe in souls or to have one.

The mechanics of diagnosis are mostly done, in my

ignorant opinion, by technicians. The technicians bring in the raw material. The doctor puts them into a poem of diagnosis. So I want a doctor with a sensibility. And that seems almost like an oxymoron, a contradiction in terms. A doctor is a man of science. Imagine having Chekhov, who was a doctor, for your doctor. Imagine having William Carlos Williams, who was a poet, or Walker Percy, who's a novelist, for your doctor. Imagine having Rabelais, who was a doctor, as your physician. My God, I could conjure with him!

Inside every patient there's a poet trying to get out. For the sick man, distance lends enchantment to life. His sickness supplies the "dissociation of sensibility" that T. S. Eliot saw as the source of modern poetry. The sick man's story and his perceptions are part of "the literature of extreme situations," a phrase that was in vogue in the 1950s and that still applies today. My ideal doctor would "read" my poetry, my literature. He would see that my sickness has purified me, weakening my worst parts and strengthening the best.

I don't see any reason why doctors shouldn't read a little poetry as part of their training. Dying or illness is a kind of poetry. It's a derangement. In literary criticism they talk about the systematic derangement of the senses. This is what happens to the sick man. So it seems to me doctors could study poetry to understand these dissociations, these derangements, and it would be a more total embracing of the patient's condition.

Of course, we used to have a priest to sit by the bedside and provide these services. Priests were learned men, so that when you said something they perhaps understood the scope of what you were saying, and then we were promised a kind of heaven or hell afterward. Once we had a narrative of heaven and hell, but now we make our own narratives. I'm making my own narrative here and now. Yet the real narrative of dying now is that you die in a machine. Kafka has a wonderful story called "The Penal Colony" in which a criminal is put in a machine that inscribes on his body with a needle the nature of his crime. We die through these machines, and that's not the right way.

I would like my doctor to understand that beneath my surface cheerfulness, I feel what Ernest Becker called "the panic inherent in creation" and "the suction of infinity." When he says, "You have prostate cancer. It has gone beyond the prostate into the rind. I think it's probably in the lymph nodes. It may be in the tailbone." Then the panic inherent in creation immediately rises up before you. I would like him to know what I mean if I told him that, like Baudelaire, "I cultivate my hysteria with joy and terror." Or if I said, like Hamlet to Horatio, "I may think meet to put an antic disposition on." My friends flatter me by calling my performance courageous or gallant, but my doctor should know better. He should be able to imagine the aloneness of the critically ill, a solitude as haunting as a Chirico painting. I want him to be my Virgil, leading me through my purgatory or inferno, pointing out the sights as we go.

My ideal doctor would resemble Oliver Sacks. I can imagine Dr. Sacks *entering* my condition, looking around at it from the inside like a kind landlord, with a tenant, trying to see how he could make the premises more livable. He would look around, holding me by the hand, and he would figure out what it feels like to be me. Then he would try to find certain advantages in the situation. He can turn disadvantages into advantages. Dr. Sacks would see the *genius* of my illness. He would mingle his daemon with mine. We would wrestle with my fate together, like Rupert and Birkin in the library in D. H. Lawrence's *Women in Love.*

In Oliver Sacks's book on hearing loss, *Seeing Voices,* he says that signing is infinitely more expressive than speech. Speech is riddled with clichés, but signing, he says, "can evoke a concreteness, a vividness, a realness, an aliveness that spoken languages, if they ever had, have long since abandoned." Once, walking along Madison Avenue, I saw two men. They happened to be black men signing to one another. It was gorgeous. It was like a dance by Merce Cunningham. A third man joined in. They were arguing. I could tell that the third man was Latin American because there was a lot of mambo in his signing.

To the typical physician, my illness is a routine incident in his rounds, while for me it's the crisis of my life. I would feel better if I had a doctor who at least perceived this incongruity. I don't ask him to love me—in fact, I think the role of love is greatly exaggerated by many writers on illness. Sick people can get sick of a love that has to be purchased for the occasion like flowers or candy brought to the hospital. Those flowers smell of pity, and only children can eat so much candy. Of course you want your family and close friends to love you, but the situation shouldn't become a hunting season for love or a competition, a desperate kiss before dying. To a critically ill person love may begin to resemble an anesthetic. In a novel by Joy Williams called *State of Grace,* a character says, "There must be something beyond love. I want to get there." The sick man has got there: He's at a point where what he wants most from people is not love but an appreciative critical grasp of his situation, what is known now in the literature of illness as "empathetic witnessing." The patient is always on the brink of revelation, and he needs an amanuensis.

I see no reason or need for my doctor to love me—nor would I expect him to suffer with me. I wouldn't demand a lot of my doctor's time: I just wish he would *brood* on my situation for perhaps five minutes, that he would give me his whole mind just once, be *bonded* with me for a brief space, survey my soul as well as my flesh, to get at my illness, for each man is ill in his own way.

I think that the doctor can keep his technical posture and still move into the human arena. The doctor can use his science as a kind of poetic vocabulary instead of using it as a piece of machinery, so that his jargon can become the jargon of a kind of poetry. I see no reason why he has to stop being a doctor and become an amateur human being. Yet many doctors systematically avoid contact. I don't expect my doctor to sound like Oliver Sacks, but I do expect some willingness to make contact, some suggestion of availability.

. . .

I would also like a doctor who *enjoyed* me. I want to be a good story for him, to give him some of my art in exchange for his. If a patient expects a doctor to be interested in him, he ought to try to *be* interesting. When he shows nothing but a greediness for care, nothing but the coarser forms of anxiety, it's only natural for the doctor to feel an aversion. There is an etiquette to being sick. I never act sick with my doctor. As I've said, I have been accelerated by my illness, and when my doctor comes in, I juggle him. I toss him about. I throw him from hand to hand, and he hardly knows what to do with me. I never act sick. A puling person is not appealing.

I have a wistful desire for our relationship to be beautiful in some way that I can't quite identify. A famous Surrealist dictum says that "Beauty is the chance meeting, on an operating table, of a sewing machine and an umbrella." Perhaps we could be beautiful like that. Just as he orders blood tests and bone scans of my body, I'd like my doctor to scan *me,* to grope for my spirit as well as my prostate. Without some such recognition, I am nothing but my illness.

While he inevitably feels superior to me because he is the doctor and I am the patient, I'd like him to know that I feel superior to him, too, that he is my patient also and I have my diagnosis of him. There should be a place where our respective superiorities could meet and frolic together. Finally, I would be happier with a witty doctor who could appreciate the comedy as well as the tragedy of my illness, its quirks and eccentricities, the final jokes of a personality that has nothing further to lose.

I find an irresistible desire to make jokes. When you're lying in the hospital with a catheter and IV in your arm, you have two choices, self-pity or irony. If the doctor doesn't get your ironies, who else is there around?

I was in a hospital room in Brigham. I was there because my catheter kept blocking. When you have a biopsy, a scab forms, and then afterward the scab breaks off, and sometimes bleeding resumes. There are clots, and the clots choke the catheter. The ordinary catheter is about the size of a soda straw. The catheter they put in me was like a garden hose. I was not comfortable.

Finally, they took out the catheter and they said, Now you'll be able to pee again. After a while I felt this Niagara-like rush mounting in me, like the rush of orgasm which you hear approaching in the distance. I leapt out of bed. I did a skip and sprinted toward the bathroom. I didn't make it. I splashed urine and blood all over the floor. My roommate, the hoodlum, who has drawn blood in anger, jumped out of bed with an expression of horror. He began mopping up the floor with a sheet. Illness is not all tragedy. Much of it is funny.

When we are seriously ill we bring our records, our medical histories, from our personal physicians to the specialist to whom we have been referred. This may tell him more about us—which vulnerabilities we have shown in the past and which capacities for resistance. The specialist learns what kind of body or system he is dealing with. He gets information that his own examination and all the machines in the hospital may not be able to give him. Since so many patients have been psychoanalyzed, or have undergone psychotherapy of some kind, I wonder whether they shouldn't bring to the specialist a brief summation of these findings, too, so that this new doctor knows *whose* body he's treating and what its spiritual composition is. How can a doctor presume to cure a patient if he knows nothing about his soul, his personality, his character disorders? It's all part of it.

When I was in my early twenties, I remember going to the therapist Ernst Schachtel and talking and talking and talking, and one day he said to me, "But what is it you want, Mister Broyard? What is it you want?" And I said, "I want to be transfigured." Well, the transfiguration is part of it. It's part of the physical, too, and I wanted to bring to my urologist the message that I wanted to be transfigured, partly by him. Why couldn't he do it, this elegant man with the tassels on his shoes? Proust said that his doctor did not take into account the fact that he had read Shakespeare. That, after all, was part of his illness. I think being a literary critic is highly carcinogenic. Have there been any studies?

Since technology deprives me of the intimacy of my illness, makes it not mine but something that belongs to science, I wish my doctor could somehow repersonalize it for me. It would be more satisfying to me, it would allow me to feel that I *owned* my illness, if my urologist were to say, "You know, you've worked this prostate of yours pretty hard. It looks like a worn-out baseball." Nobody wants an anonymous illness. I'd much rather think that I brought it on myself than that it was a mere accident of nature. In *The Sorcerers of Dobu,* Reo Fortune pointed out that each man in the Dobuan tribe "owned" several diseases, such as tertiary yaws, incontinence of semen, and elephantiasis of the scrotum. These were his patrimony, which he used as curses or weapons in defending himself against his enemies. If I "own" my disease, perhaps I too can conjure with it, even use it against itself.

It is only natural for a patient to feel some disgust at the changes brought about in his body by illness, and I wonder whether an innovative doctor couldn't find a way to reconceptualize this situation. For example, when we are caught up in sexual desire we lose much of our squeamishness about the body, and perhaps there is some way for the doctor to enable the patient to sexualize his illness, to treat it rather like a metasexual encounter, or even a grand masturbation, that has gone wrong or too far. The reconciling metaphor needn't be sexual. The doctor could use almost anything: "Art burned up your body with beauty and truth." Or "You've spent your self like a philanthropist who gives all his money away." If the patient can feel that he has *earned* his illness—that his sickness represents the grand decadence that follows a great flowering—he may look upon the ruin of his body as tourists look upon the great ruins of antiquity. Of course I'm offering these suggestions playfully, not so much as practical expedients but as experiments in thinking about medicine. Just as researchers play with possibilities in laboratories, medical thinking might benefit from more free association.

Physicians have been taught in medical school that they must keep the patient at a distance because there isn't time to accommodate his personality, or because if the doctor becomes *involved* in the patient's predicament, the emotional burden will be too great. As I've suggested, it doesn't take much time to make good contact, but beyond that, the emotional burden of *avoiding* the patient may be much harder on the doctor than he imagines. It may be this that sometimes makes him complain of feeling harassed. A doctor's job would be so much more interesting and satisfying if he simply let himself plunge into the patient, if he could lose his own fear of falling.

The connotation of going beyond the science into the person is all I'm asking—that there be a sign of willingness, more than a kind of Pascal-like dialogue, which is too much to ask. It could be done almost in pantomime. There is the way a doctor looks at you. One doctor I saw had a trick way of almost crossing his eyes, so he seemed to be peering warmly, humanistically, into my eyes, but he wasn't seeing me at all. He was looking without looking. I never felt that I contacted him. When I went to Schachtel for psychotherapy, instead of having me lie on a couch so that I was looking at the ceiling with him behind me, he sat across a table and we talked. He did not wish to make any eye contact because he felt if we did that while I was talking, his eyes would show, or I would imagine they were showing, approval or disapproval. So for fifty minutes while I talked he avoided my eyes.

And if our eyes did meet he would start back as though I had touched him in the genitals. I think doctors have something like this, a systematic avoidance of that click of contact.

Other doctors give you a generic, unfocused gaze. They look at you panoramically. They don't see you in focus. They look all around you, and you are a figure in the ground. You are like one of those lonely figures in early landscape painting, a figure in the distance only to give scale. If he could gaze directly at the patient, the doctor's work would be more gratifying. Why bother with sick people, why try to save them, if they're not worth acknowledging? When a doctor refuses to acknowledge a patient, he is, in effect, abandoning him to his illness.

A hospital is full of wonderful and terrible stories, and if I were a doctor I would read them as one reads good fiction and let them educate me. I'll give just one example of what I mean. A friend of mine, a writer, was dying in a hospital of lung cancer, and before he died he wanted to marry the woman he had been living with. It was not exactly a sentimental gesture; they had ceased being lovers and had become roommates. But he wanted to leave her his apartment, which was rent-controlled. He felt that she deserved it for her faithful attendance at the hospital and it was only by marrying her that he could pass it on.

He had told me this before he lost the power of speech as the result of a stroke suffered during an exploratory operation. He had also specified that I was not to arrange the marriage until I saw that his case was hopeless. When I saw his time approaching, I went out as he had asked me to and found a rabbi. The rabbi was a rather fussy intellectual with a university air, and he quizzed me at length about my friend's religious convictions. I could say only that he had written exclusively about Jewish characters and the kind of sorrows traditionally associated with them. He asked me whether the bride was a practicing Jew, and I replied that, in my opinion, she practiced unconsciously.

Grudgingly the rabbi agreed to come to the hospital and perform the ceremony. My friend was in a ward with eight beds. The other seven were occupied by Latin Americans, and salsa blared from their radios all day long. There was a continual stream of visitors, all speaking Spanish at top speed.

The rabbi was upset by the salsa, but he pulled the curtains around the bed and began the ceremony. He had been chanting in Hebrew for only a minute or two when a young doctor who had been treating my friend burst through the curtains. He seemed to think that we were encroaching on his jurisdiction, although we had already been granted permission by the head of the ward. When he understood that a wedding was taking place, the doctor leaned over my friend, who had been speechless for more than two weeks, and asked him in a loud, hectoring voice, "Do you love this woman? Do you want to marry this woman?"

Here was a doctor intervening in someone's life without understanding anything about it. If he had known his patient, he might have appreciated the pathos of the scene, for which the salsa supplied an obbligato. But he saw nothing, understood nothing.

In her essay "On Being Ill," Virginia Woolf wondered why we don't have a greater literature of illness. The answer may be that doctors discourage our stories.

Applying to other friends, following new recommendations, I found another urologist. He's brilliant, famous, a star, and my response to him was so positive that my cancer immediately went into remission. My only regret is that he doesn't talk very much—and when he does, he sounds like everybody else. His brilliance has no voice, at least not when he's with me.

This doctor is the most famous authority on the prostate in Cambridge, Massachusetts, which is crowded with doctors. He knows all there is to know about the prostate, but I cannot sit down and have a talk with him about it, which I find a very great deprivation. I remember a wonderful novel called *The Dogs of March* in which a character was a mechanic and had a son who wasn't interested in what he was interested in. At one point he said, "It is one of the great hopes of my life that someday my son and I can sit down and have a long talk about tires, automobile tires." I would like to sit down with my doctor and talk to him about the prostate. What a curious organ. What can God have been thinking when he designed it this way? I would like to have a meditation, a rumination, a lucubration, a bombination, about the prostate. I can't do it. I'm forced to stop people on the street and talk to them about it.

There's a paradox here at the heart of medicine, because a doctor, like a writer, must have a voice of his own, something that conveys the timbre, the rhythm, the diction, and the music of his humanity that compensates us for all the speechless machines. When a doctor makes a difficult diagnosis, it is not only his medical knowledge that determines it but a voice in his head. Such a diagnosis depends as much on inspiration as art does. Whether he wants to be or not, the doctor is a storyteller, and he can turn our lives into good or bad stories, regardless of the diagnosis. If my doctor would allow me, I would be glad to help him here, to take him on as *my* patient.

Although I don't expect to die for some time, my urologist is young and I see us as joined till death do us part. We will go through this together. Sometime in the future, in the neighborhood of years, when my doctor's hair has turned gray and he has had intimations of mortality, I'll die with him. Since I think of him as a star, I will not "fall as apples fall, without astronomy," as Wallace Stevens put it. We are what the French call *un couple malade,* a marriage of doctor and patient. Perhaps later, when he is older, he'll have learned how to converse. Astute as he is, he doesn't yet understand that all cures are partly "talking cures," in Freud's phrase. Every patient needs mouth-to-mouth resuscitation, for talk is the kiss of life. Besides talking himself, the doctor ought to bleed the patient of talk, of the consciousness of his illness, as earlier physicians used to bleed their patients to let out heat or dangerous humors.

Yet it's too easy to accuse the doctor, to blame the absence of natural talk on him. It's also true that much of what the patient asks is ineffable. Even Chekhov would be hard put to answer him. For example, I would like to discuss my prostate with my urologist not as a diseased organ but as a philosopher's stone. Since science tells us that energy cannot be lost in the universe, I want to ask him where, if the treatment blocks my prostate, my sexual energy goes. Could I turn it around on the disease, like a cornered rat? Would he agree that my life now is a balancing between yes and no? Is there an Ur-desire, an archaeology of passion that antedates or supersedes the prostate? Why do I sometimes feel that I'd like to excrete this unfaithful organ?

In asking such unanswerable questions, I'm no exception. Every patient invites the doctor to combine the role of the priest, the philosopher, the poet, the lover. He expects the doctor to evaluate his entire life, like a biographer. The sick man asks far too much, he is *im*patient in everything, and his doctor may be afraid of making a fool of himself in trying to reply. Each of us is a specialist in one field only.

Of course a physician may reasonably ask: "But what am I supposed to say? All I can tell the patient is the facts, if there are any facts." But this is not quite true. The doctor's answer to his patient is yet to be born. It will come naturally, or at first unnaturally, from the intersecting of the patient's needs with the doctor's experience and his as-yet-untried imagination. He doesn't have to lie to the sick man or give him false assurances: He himself, his presence, and his will to reach the patient are the assurance the sick man needs. Just as a mother ushers her child into the world, so the doctor must usher the patient out of the world of the healthy and into whatever physical and mental purgatory awaits him. The doctor is the patient's only familiar in a foreign country.

Perhaps there should be still another specialist—a combination of soothsayer, clown, and poet—to help answer the patient's questions. He could accompany the doctor on his rounds, give a second opinion. In fact, Norman Cousins does something like this. But the trouble with such an arrangement is that it leaves the doctor out. It abandons him to his own sickness, his pathological separation from the patient, his sense of an uncompleted gestalt. He turns into a machine, clanking in a void. The patient's questions still thunder in his stethoscope, for they are an integral part of the illness. The patient is suffering from terminal interrogativeness, his soul is fibrillating.

To help the doctor reach the patient, and to help the patient reach the doctor, the mood of the hospital might have to be modified. It ought to be less like a laboratory and more like a theater, which would be only fitting, since no place contains more drama. The laboratory atmosphere can probably be traced back to the idea of asepsis, to the avoidance of contagion. Originally, the patient was protected by the sterility of the hospital. Only the sterility went too far: It sterilized the doctor's thinking. It sterilized the patient's entire experience in the hospital. It sterilized the very notion of illness to the point where we can't bring our soiled thoughts to bear on it. But the sick man needs the contagion of life. Death is the ultimate sterility.

I found an interesting exception to this distance between the doctor and the patient. It was in the emergency room of a hospital, of all places. After the cystoscopy my catheter had become blocked, in the middle of the night, by blood clots, and I was in considerable discomfort. I felt that I might actually explode. I called the covering urologist, and he advised me to go to the emergency room and have the catheter flushed out. When I arrived I was received with warm sympathy by a young intern and a beautiful nurse, who between them flushed out my catheter not once, but half a dozen times, just to make sure. They listened appreciatively to my dithyrambic account of what it felt like to empty my bladder. While the nurse was tenderly adjusting the tape that held the catheter tube to my thigh, the supervising physician came in. He had recognized my name from seeing it in the paper I work for and said he was glad to meet me.

I was almost dizzy with relief and gratitude, thanking everyone three or four times, shaking hands left and right. It was not until much later that I figured out what had made the atmosphere here so different from the usual hospital scene. I think it was because this was the *emergency* room, in the front lines of medicine. These doctors and nurses still saw illness as an emergency, an emotional crisis. Also, they would meet me only once: I was a novelty, there was no question of their being permanently saddled with me. Every case in the emergency room is, in this sense, unique—and this allows the staff to be natural. There is no bureaucracy: I was not so much a patient as a needy person coming in from the street. For all its occasional horrors, the emergency room is like a medical game, a continual improvisation.

Not every patient can be saved, but his illness may be eased by the way the doctor responds to him—and in responding to him the doctor may save himself. But first he must become a student again; he has to dissect the cadaver of his professional persona; he must see that his silence and neutrality are *unnatural.* It may be necessary to give up some of his authority in exchange for his humanity, but as the old family doctors knew, this is not a bad bargain. In learning to talk to his patients, the doctor may talk himself back into loving his work. He has little to lose and everything to gain by letting the sick man into his heart. If he does, they can share, as few others can, the wonder, terror, and exaltation of being on the edge of being, between the natural and the supernatural.

When Anatole gave a talk at the University of Chicago Medical School in April of 1990 to a group assembled under the aegis of the medical ethics seminar, members of the audience wanted to know if he had found the doctor he was looking for. He answered by saying, "My urologist is a very handsome man. He's slender and a fabled tennis player. He wears very expensive loafers and has a sixty-dollar haircut. He comes into the room like a bullfighter. He has style. He has magic and is extremely competent. He doesn't talk. He's too much of a star, but he has an oncologist who talks for him."

PART FOUR

JOURNAL NOTES

May-September, 1990

BEING ILL AND DYING is largely, to a great degree, a matter of style. My intention is to show people who are ill—and we will all be ill someday—that it's not the end of their world as they know it, that they can go on being themselves, perhaps even more so than before. They can make a game, a career, even an art form of opposing their illness. There are so many interesting and therapeutic things they can do. It's not enough to be "positive," brave, or stoical: These are too simple, like New Year's resolutions.

We should break down the idea of "the will to live" into more palatable components, into insights and tactics that appeal not only to the man of average sensibility but to skeptical, ironical people. In a sense, illness is a drug, and it's partly up to the patient to determine whether it will be a low or a high.

I would advise every sick person to evolve a style or develop a voice for his or her illness. In my own case I make fun of my illness. I disparage it. This wasn't a deliberate decision; the response simply came to me. Adopting a style for your illness is another way of meeting it on your own grounds, of making it a mere character in your narrative.

One of the things I think the patient has to avoid is developing a false self. If you try to seduce your doctor by being particularly nice, then you become untrue to yourself and you develop a false self with the doctor, which is very damaging. You must remain yourself. Of course, if you remain yourself with the doctor, he may not like it. Doctors are used to having patients offer them false selves, but I think that doctors have to be taught to recognize and accept the patient's true self.

When you're ill you instinctively fear a diminishment and disfigurement of yourself. It's that, more than dying, that frightens you. You're going to become a monster. I think you have to develop a style when you're ill to keep from falling out of love with yourself. It's important to stay in love with yourself. That's known as the will to live. And your style is the instrument of your vanity. If they can afford it, I think it would be good therapy, good body narcissism, for cancer patients to buy a whole new wardrobe, mostly elegant, casual clothes.

Anxiety is the cancer patient's worst enemy. It reminds me of a catheter, which all prostate cancers require at some point. Anxiety is like a catheter inserted in your soul, and if the patient can get on better terms with his anxiety, he'll feel something like the relief I felt when the doctor pulled the catheter out of my penis and urethral canal. I've been studying anxiety for many years—it's my hobby—and I've learned that it can sometimes be turned around and made into a kind of a pet, like a dog, or an amusing Kafkaesque companion.

The sick person's best medicine is desire—the desire to live, to be with other people, to do things, to get back to his life. When I was in the hospital, I was always gazing out of the window at the real world, which had never looked more desirable. I'd like to suggest, to invent or imagine or recall, ways of keeping one's desire alive as a way of keeping oneself alive.

I really think you have to have a style in which you finish your life. That's what I'm doing right now. I'm finishing my life. I think one ought to die at a kind of party, the way Socrates died. All of his disciples came to his bedside. When André Gide was dying, he was surrounded by friends and journalists. Gide was a very compulsive man. He used to play the piano without touching the keys because he was afraid that someone might hear him making a mistake. So, when he died, his last words were to the journalists: "Before you quote me, make sure I'm conscious." He wanted to die in his own style, and that seems to me quite reasonable. I think in the last stage of dying the doc-

tor should be removed and so too the grisly Elisabeth
Kübler-Ross, who actually wrote to the parents of a child
who had died saying how much she had enjoyed participat-
ing in the event. I would like to die in my own way. It's
my house, my life, my death, my friends. Why not?

A critically ill person ought to be entitled to anything
that affords him relief. While Byron's Sardanapalus went too
far in condemning his concubines, his slaves, his horses and
dogs, to die with him, one can understand the impulse. A
better way, I think, would be for the patient to write a last will
and testament, summing up his satisfactions and regrets, de-
scribing his loves in lyrical, even pornographic, detail and his
hatreds too in all their vehemence, as a kind of final settling
of unfinished business. A last will and testament would be like
a final disinhibiting, fuller than the one-sided deathbed confes-
sion to a priest. It would be a period to the long sentence of
life. Cranked up in his bed like Sardanapalus, the patient
could bestow symbolic life and death, in his own heart at least,
among his intimates. He could leave the legacy of his true
feelings.

There comes a point where it's pretty obvious that a
patient is going to die, and I think to eke out a few more days
by mechanical means is a mistake, and I think that the patient
should be allowed to glide or skate or dance into death in the
way that he chooses rather than be ministered to until the last

minute, which I think is obscene. You know when a patient is moribund, and then you leave him alone. You let him die in his own way, and you let him make his final arrangements unimpeded by technology.

I liked it when people died of brain fever. What a wonderful thing to die of. I once asked my father, "How did your father die?" His father was a famous man in New Orleans. His nickname was Belle Homme, beautiful man. Half the people in New Orleans were bastards of his who all took our name, and finally, at the age of eighty-seven, he died. It was a hot night in August. He ate a dozen bananas, and he took a cold bath. What a great way to die.

Any meaning of illness is better than none.

Philippe Ariès, in his book *The Hour of Our Death,* says that there are good deaths, there are beautiful deaths, there are untamed deaths, there are tame deaths. I want an untamed, beautiful death. So I think that we should have a competition in dying, sort of like Halloween costumes. If you have to die, and I hope you don't, I think you should try to die the most beautiful death you can. Let's give a prize for the most beautiful death. We can call it heaven.

I don't really know how much my mind can do to help me out in my illness. Maybe it can't do anything. Maybe these are just the patient's delusions of grandeur. But the delusions of grandeur of the patient are therapeutic. I give in to them.

The doctor has the impossible job of trying to reconcile the patient to illness and dying.

Technical explanations flatten the story of illness.

There has been insomnia: as if I couldn't turn off my sense of time, couldn't stop thinking of all that I wanted to do. Perhaps, like the child's prayer, I thought that I would die before I woke. My life has become a vigil.

I don't need sleep. I live on excitement.

There is a time of the night between midnight and dawn when people despair.

What is my doctor thinking as he says, "You have six to eighteen months"? I ask him about other patients, successes for his sake.

Isn't there some way to turn dying into some kind of celebration, a birthday to end all birthdays?

You mustn't surrender to illness: Shave, comb your hair, dress attractively, be aggressive, not passive. It's the change in the sick person that embarrasses his friends, and the whole inhibition begins there.

All my friends are wits, but now that I'm sick I'm treated to the spectacle of watching them wear different faces. They come to see me and instead of being ironical and making jokes, they're terribly serious. They look at me with a kind of grotesque lovingness in their faces. They touch me. They feel my pulse almost. They're trying to give me their strength, and I'm trying to shove it off.

The dying man has to decide how tactful he wants to be.

What a critically ill person needs above all is to be understood. Dying is a misunderstanding you have to get straightened out before you go. And you can't be understood, your situation can't be appreciated, until your family and friends, staring at you with an embarrassed love, know—with an intimate, absolute knowledge—what your illness is like.

At the end, you're posing for eternity. It's your last picture. Don't be carried into death. Leap into it.

I wouldn't call my attitude courageous. I'd call it irresponsible.

.   .   .

Illness is a kind of incoherence. I could only become coherent if I were to get well or if I were to die, so I'm condemned to some kind of incoherence.

There is sudden pathos. I had seemed to friends and acquaintances to be good for another twenty years. They found a dying Anatole easier to like, more interesting. I have become a ghost who is at the same time more real than they are. I have lost my remorselessness. I find it difficult to be serious, to give up a lifetime habit of irony.

Why did all this wisdom and beauty have to come so late?

One last spray of personality.

The dying man has to decide how tactful he wants to be.

The important thing is the patient, not the treatment.

PART FIVE

THE LITERATURE
OF DEATH

1981-1982

THE LITERATURE OF DEATH

I

IN THE 1960s, books told us how to rescue our identities from their crises, how to "realize" ourselves, how to ramify our sexual behavior. In the seventies and eighties, there has been a wave of books telling us how to die. Our anxiety has advanced from incidentals to ultimates; in our impatience we have run through life and arrived at death, which would seem to be our "accelerated grimace."

For a while in this century dying was such a forbidden subject, such a suppressed excitement, that Geoffrey Gorer wrote an essay called "The Pornography of Death." Now we may be carrying the pornography to the other extreme, to morbid exhibitionism and "the thrill of death." We take lessons in dying, as we take lessons in giving birth, or as we pose, or compose, ourselves for a photograph, which Roland Barthes in his "Camera Lucida" calls a micro-version of death.

In *The Hour of Our Death,* Philippe Ariès speaks of "tame death," in which the support and participation of the community integrate dying into the flow of life. The authority and presence of the community soften the impact of death, for the most wistful word in thanatology is "alone."

By the seventeenth century, in Ariès's reckoning, people began to worry rather obsessively about their mortality, as they have done ever since. They began to protest it as if it were *un*natural, an obscene prank of nature. "Death untamed" was seen not as a completion but a contradiction of life, an unceremonious erasing of the individual. The community turned its back, and the dying man faced his terrible adversary on his own.

In the "beautiful death" of the nineteenth century, Ariès suggests, the drama of isolated, unsupported dying led to its being romanticized. Romanticism has always loved the dying fall, the morbid frisson, and the ineffable. Death, in fact, is Romanticism's favorite metaphor, the grand scene or climax of life. Grief and tragedy are confused, and as Mario Praz might say, death becomes the ultimate Romantic agony.

With the twentieth century we arrive at what Ariès calls "dirty," "obscene," or "invisible" death, an event which occurs in the interstices of technology. The current spate of books about death, he contends, represents our attempt to control its reawakened "wildness."

Not every writer on death shares this bleak view. For all his brilliant erudition, Ariès may be something of a Romantic himself on the subject of death. The best French social scientists all have something of the *poète manqué,* even *maudit,* about them.

At the opposite end of the spectrum is Elisabeth Kübler-Ross, one of the pioneers of positive thanatology, whose work has been a lifelong effort to demystify and domesticate death. In *Living with Death and Dying,* Dr. Kübler-Ross asks for screaming rooms where patients can retire to screech or howl their protest against pain, separation, and the interruption of their lives. She believes that even mutilated or disfigured bodies should be viewed so that there will be no mystery, no ambiguity. In her single-minded dedication, she is sometimes a bit grotesque.

Though Dr. Kübler-Ross does not have a graceful style or a talent for imagery—her prose, in fact, has something of a death grip about it—her book is filled with poignant first-hand material. A young woman who never has visitors picks up the telephone beside her bed in the hospital and listens to the dial tone "just to hear a sound." A hostile wife, bringing visitors to her dying husband's bedside, gives his cheek a cruel admonitory pinch and cries, "Be sociable!"

In *Death as a Fact of Life,* David Hendin maintains that a good death is an indispensable end to a good life, so much so that a German writer referred to the final moments as "the obstetrics of the soul." To die well is important not only to the patient but to his survivors, for one of their strongest memories of him may be what Walter Benjamin called "love at last sight."

Death is the source of some of our best images, and Mr.

Hendin's book contains some striking ones. During the eighteenth century, he writes, when science was becoming self-important, there was some dispute about the criteria for death, and various "life tests" were devised. In one of these the doctor blew a trumpet—the last trump—in the patient's face: If he did not respond, he was assumed to be dead. One imagines the doctor in his wig, knee britches, and flared coat picking up the unfamiliar instrument. His conception of the trumpet derives from Bach and Handel, who used it to celebrate the afterlife. But his purpose is quite different; he brings the instrument to his lips in order to interrogate this life.

II

While books have always tried to show us how to live, they are trying now to teach us how to die. The fascination with nothingness that we find in contemporary philosophy, fiction, and painting seems to have been extended to the nothingness beyond death, and we have developed a literature that tries to soften the impact of that impending nothingness.

For all the eloquence of the books about death, the imagery evoked in the dying person by the event itself is surprisingly meager. In *Between Life and Death,* edited by Robert Kastenbaum, a writer named Garfield summarizes his conversations with terminal cancer patients, who told him of their "altered state" experiences on the brink of death. According to him, they fall into four groups: those who report a powerful white light and celestial music, as well as an encounter with a religious figure or a deceased relative; those who are confronted by demonic figures or nightmarish presences; those who are aware of dreamlike images, either blissful or terrifying; and those who feel themselves to be entering a void or tunnel.

If this is true—and several other investigators report similar findings—then the vocabulary of death is anticlimactic. It seems that we die in clichés.

Some accounts of the experience of dying are almost comical in their complacency. A Swiss geology professor named Heim collected reports of climbers who had survived near-fatal falls in the Alps. While they believed they were falling to their death, Mr. Heim says, not one of the many people he interviewed succumbed to fear, despair, or anxiety. Rather, they felt a calm, profound acceptance, an enhanced, accelerated awareness, and a greatly expanded sense of time.

In *Between Life and Death,* Robert Kastenbaum is skeptical about the sentimentality of some accounts of death and the benign tenor of others. He feels that the "thrill of death" approach encourages would-be suicides. And indeed suicide is also developing a literature, including books such as *Suicide: The Philosophical Issues,* edited by M. Pabst Battin and David J. Mayo. Some of the arguments advanced in favor of suicide can be read as part of a growing tendency to try to wrest death from nature and bring it under man's control.

In *The Human Encounter with Death,* Stanislav Brof and Joan Halifax describe their use of LSD-assisted psychotherapy in helping terminal cancer patients to overcome their pain, depression, and withdrawal through something like an orgasm of consciousness. One of the great pities of death is that people so often *shrink* into it, and the authors reason that it would be better for the patient to *burst* into it, to experience death as an ecstasy, as Christian martyrs were said to have done.

Though some patients had "bad trips" even under controlled conditions after taking hallucinogens, others who had been stunned by pain and dread are described as talking freely, even joyously, with friends and relatives. In what the literature might call an authenticating emotional closure, they reviewed or relived the lives they were about to leave. But while for some people this may seem an ideal way to die, for others it will be interpreted as tampering with or trivializing the most solemn moment of our experience.

As he lay dying, Tolstoy said, "I don't understand what I'm supposed to do." In the past decade the literature of death has been trying to answer his questions.

DOMESTICATING DEATH

Understanding death and coming to terms with it may turn out to be one of our major achievements in the twentieth century. In the last ten years, there has been an enormous literature of death, and in a sense, Lisl Goodman's *Death and the Creative Life* is like the concluding chapter of that literature.

What she offers is a means, an attitude, a technique, even, for domesticating death, for living comfortably and intimately with it. This is not as gruesome as it may sound; in fact, her book goes a long way toward eliminating the gruesomeness of death.

A practicing psychoanalyst and a teacher, Miss Goodman, assisted by her students, systematically interviewed almost seven hundred people on the subject of death. They ranged from some of the foremost artists and scientists of our time to people at various levels of success and self-realization to those who saw themselves as failures dragging out wasted lives.

Right at the beginning of her research, she discovered a curious reaction—all but one of the famous female artists she wrote to refused to see her. Because it was part of her plan to compare artists and scientists, she was forced to abandon famous female scientists. With a charming bluntness, Miss Goodman says she cannot explain the women's refusals.

"I don't think people are afraid of death. What they are afraid of is the incompleteness of their life." Made by a 30-year-old man who was dying of leukemia, this statement is at the core of Miss Goodman's approach to the subject. Because our longevity potential is about 150 years, we almost always die prematurely, she says, and that is one of the ironies of life.

She suggests, however, another kind of reckoning, substituting the idea of completeness for longevity, which is only a temporal completeness. If we live fully, Miss Goodman argues, death comes to feel natural to us as a part of the life process, instead of seeming to be an "absurd" interruption. Starting with the proposition that we appreciate life most ardently when we are about to lose it, she reasons that a full acknowledgment of death would encourage us to value every moment of life.

Although it has long been a commonplace, going back to Lucretius and Montaigne, that life is the answer to death, Miss Goodman has advanced this from an aphorism to a strategy. The twenty-two artists and scientists who are the main focus of her book do not seem to fear death, both because they are too immersed in living and because they feel that they have "completed" themselves.

She finds that successful artists rate death positively and scientists rate it "slightly negatively." The lower the sense of fulfillment, she writes, the more negative is the rating given to death by the subject—and to life as well. Although no artists interviewed see death as cruel, half the scientists do. The violinist Isaac Stern compares his feelings toward death to the tension before a performance. "Solitary" is the wistful word used by most subjects about death.

"Fame asserts existence," Miss Goodman writes, echoing Ernest Becker's theory that a striving for some sort of immortality is our basic motivating impulse, as well as our best defense against death. "I love my work," most of the successful artists and scientists say, suggesting that love, too, is an answer to death. "Whatever you really want," one scientist says, "you must want it irrationally."

Miss Goodman, who has an adventurous mind, distinguishes between an internal and an external expectation of death. Quoting Georg Simmel, who observed that in Shakespeare, subordinate characters succumb to external forces while tragic heroes "are allowed to die from within," she urges us to take death in, even to learn to love it as the final reward for all our striving toward completeness. One of her boldest suggestions is that we reckon our age by counting not from birth forward, but from death backward, based on how much life we realistically estimate we have left to us. In this way, we would keep life, and death, always in front of us.

Though *Death and the Creative Life* is not thick in pages, it is thick with ideas, with life, and with hope. In the inspired way she thinks, Miss Goodman illustrates her own assertion that we are never so much alive as when we are in the presence of death.

LIFE BEFORE DEATH

Good books should be revisited, just as we revisit places or paintings or listen again to a piece of music. I've usually found that a second reading of a good book is even better than the first, because this time you're prepared for it, like someone who stretches and limbers up before exercising. Though the pleasure is just as great, it's more of a conscious pleasure than a blind surrender. You're more alert to what is happening.

For example, I've just reread Ernest Becker's *The Denial of Death,* and I'm surprised at how new it seems to me, perhaps because I have changed since I first read it in 1974, when it was published. Though the book won the Pulitzer Prize and was well reviewed, I've never felt that it received the attention it deserved or that it was as widely read or influential as it should have been. While it is used in colleges, I hardly ever hear of anyone but a student, or Annie Hall in the Woody Allen film, reading it.

The Denial of Death is a state-of-the-union message about the human psyche, as well as a survey and synthesis of the main currents of psychoanalytic thought. Mr. Becker's view of human nature is romantic, as opposed to the rather dismaying "classical" school centered on Freud or the sentimental exhortations of what might be called the California, or encounter, school. Although I'm attracted by the ironies and the tragic flair of Freud's ideas, there's a rather plaintive voice inside me that wants to know why the analysis of the human soul should not be a romantic affair, that argues that men and women are the only romantic animals in creation, that it's our redeeming feature. To be conscious, to love, to strive, to write poetry or music, to be aware of death—what else is this but romantic?

It is not, Mr. Becker says, our desire to sleep with our mothers and slay our fathers that drives us but a wish to be our own fathers, to wrest the self from the history of the family and project it into immortality. We defend ourselves not against castration anxiety but against death, a far more absolute castration. How can we achieve immortality? According to Mr. Becker, by becoming so insistently and inimitably ourselves, or by producing something so indelibly our own, that we may be said, as a poet put it, to have added forever to the sum of reality.

Of course, most of us must necessarily fail in this attempt, but it is something worthwhile and interesting to do with ourselves, much better than trying to sleep with our mothers, worrying about our genitalia, or approaching our personalities as if they were mere issues of civil or sexual liberty. Mr. Becker asks us to be, or to try to be, heroic, and while this is a large order, it can be argued that we are constitutionally pointed in that direction. Also, it would seem that life is hardly worth all the anxiety, the frustration, and the inevitable humiliation unless there is a hope of glory. Our movement toward glory may be a response to what Mr. Becker calls the suction of infinity, which I take to be a rather sophisticated substitute for the traditional notion of heaven.

This is ripe stuff indeed, almost a kind of cosmic pep talk, but all the same we've been going in for this sort of thing since the beginning of civilization, and at least Mr. Becker offers his suggestions in concrete and potentially satisfying form. Love, "a cosmology of two," is one of the death-defying heroisms, a hugging of another person as if he or she were not only a body but the embodiment of a principle. Group behavior is a "timid heroism," a reluctance to emerge from what Ernst Schachtel calls "embeddedness."

Quoting Philip Rieff, Mr. Becker describes character as "a restrictive shaping of possibility." The great problem in life is how much to restrict and how much possibility to risk. There is, Mr. Becker says, "a panic inherent in creation," and we have to control that panic without tranquilizing it. We have to convert it into usable excitement, what some writers would call creativity.

One of our difficulties is that we feel that "the heroic seems too big for us, or we too small for it." Human heroics are "a blind drivenness that burns people up; in passionate people, a screaming of glory as uncritical and reflexive as the howling of a dog." Embarrassed by this natural exhibitionism, most of us tend to subdue our sense of ecstasy or grandeur, to inhibit our private madness and call it sanity, to live out our lives incognito, concealing our true selves even from ourselves.

Contemporary man, Mr. Becker believes, has been alienated by his own analytic powers to the point where he is in danger of only "playing at the meaning of life." Yet the author is the first to admit that heroism is risky, because a full apprehension of the human condition might be more than we could bear. For all his romanticism, his belief in the necessity of the heroic, Mr. Becker's concluding statement is surprisingly modest: "The most that any of us can seem to do is to fashion something—an object, or ourselves—and drop it into the confusion, make an offering of it, so to speak, to the life force."

That doesn't sound impossible. If I were you, I'd buy a paperback copy of *The Denial of Death* and then go out and try to get myself some glory.

A STYLE FOR DEATH

I sometimes wonder how much the act of writing means to the novelist and how it connects him to his life, or perhaps to his death. I was given one kind of answer to this question when a close friend of mine, a writer named Paul Breslow, died of cancer in August. He spent his last three or four months trying to finish a novel, and in talking to him about his book, his life, and his death, I learned quite a lot about how they fitted together.

Though he had published stories, articles, and reviews, and had written with his wife, Kay, a book on architecture, Paul felt that unless he completed his novel he would be a failure—he wouldn't have done anything. While I had some doubts about his ability, in his condition, to bring the book to a close, I saw it as a project that might occupy his days and nights with something other than pain and dread, and so I encouraged him.

Imagine a man in a hospital bed, regularly racked by spasms, unable to sit up or move, looking death in the face at the age of forty-seven—imagine such a man trying to write a witty, metaphysical novel. Though the anesthetic he was given suppressed only a small part of the pain—just enough to keep him from screaming—it made him drowsy, and he fought the drowsiness by taking several Ritalin tablets a day. His heart had never been strong, and so much Ritalin was dangerous for him, but as he said to me, with a smile that comprehended everything, "I don't think this is a time for caution."

While I could understand his desire to finish his book, I argued with him about calling himself a failure if he couldn't do it. He had led what seemed to me a wonderful life, traveling extensively and living abroad, making nineteen trips, for example, into the African bush to collect primitive sculpture, and in general following the impulses of his sensibility. Since he had enough money, he passed his days reading and became the most interestingly, if not the most exhaustively, educated man I knew. His manners were so exquisite that they were like a definition of civilization.

"To be what you are, who you are," I said to him, "can't be called a failure. If I admire you," I said rather immodestly, "how can you be a failure? In fact," I added, "you're the only person I know with whom I can have exalted conversations without feeling self-conscious." No, he objected, only a novel could justify his forty-seven years. I think he saw this novel of his as some sort of return or reciprocal payment for the rather privileged life he'd had.

On a contraption suspended over his bed, he wrote lying

down, his hand moving very slowly because of his illness. It felt odd, he said, to write in a horizontal position, and he wondered whether it would make his sentences sound passive or labored or idle. He had an extremely complex style, one that depended on a most precise diction and on rhythms that told the reader how to inflect that diction. While I naturally expected him to foreshorten his book and hurry it to a close, he kept expanding it, adding further dimensions to what was already an intricate structure. He played with writing, reveled in it, as if he were having a last fling. Perhaps he pretended to himself that so long as he was still inventing he couldn't die.

He seemed to think that nothing but a novel—not non-fiction, because it was too detached, or poetry, because it was too fragmented—could notify the world of who or what he was, or had been. We talked about death, and I asked him whether there was some final statement other than his pro-jected book that he felt impelled to make. I had always sup-posed that if I were dying, I'd want to sum up somehow. He thought for a moment and then answered, with his habitually self-deprecating smile, "I'm not sure there is any statement to make. One doesn't want to die." He always used "one" when he felt that "I" might sound melodramatic.

From all the books he'd read, Paul distilled a style for his death. There wasn't a bad sentence in his last hundred days. He revised his dying before he spoke to me about it, and sometimes I chafed at this restraint. I yearned to say some-thing passionate, but I could never make up my mind whether I had the right to impose my passion on him. I may even have become jealous of his focusing so intensely on writing: I wanted him to know that he was leaving me, his friendship with me, incomplete, too. He often talked of inconveniencing me by causing me to come to the hospital, and at last I burst out that it was far more inconvenient for me to lose one of the rare persons I loved.

In a sense Paul had disciplined himself to treat his death as a kind of literature, and this made it easier for him to bear. He turned it into irony, but I was not fooled. Irony is something you can carry off only when you have an audience. When there was no one with him, when he was alone in his hospital room, I suspect that he was what a poet called "a spirit storming in blank walls."

Though he covered quite a few pages with his slackening fingers, he never finished his novel, never reached that final satisfaction. He was anything but a failure, though, because the style is the man and literature isn't everything.

PART SIX

WHAT THE CYSTOSCOPE SAID

I read where you don't suffer comforters lightly, but I have to tell you I was shocked to read about your cancer. It doesn't pay to write a wonderful story like "What the Cystoscope Said," not so long as Aristophanes is God.

FROM A LETTER FROM PHILIP ROTH

Life can only be understood backward.

KIERKEGAARD

W H E N   I   S A W my father with the horse collar around his neck, I knew immediately. I didn't admit it until much later, but there was never any doubt in my mind.

Some people are just stopped dead in their tracks, as though the reel had broken—their last image lingers in the mind's eye, and they never completely die—but my father was demoted down the evolutionary scale into nothingness. He lost position after position in an interminable retreat. Just as he had been at first conceived, he was at last deconceived, and like a child who takes apart a favorite toy, impelled by some insatiable love, I watched his inner workings come loose and found out what made him tick. Then, as now, I felt that this was most natural. The relation between a son and father *ought to be* barbaric.

The stiff neck came from pulling up roots. After sixty years of deferring pleasures, he'd finally bought a little house in the country. He was pampering it when it got him in the neck. The irony was so pat that it made you feel he wasn't significant enough to rate a more elaborate twist. "You must have slept in a draft," my mother said, and she rubbed him with liniment and wrapped his neck with flannel. "You must have strained yourself," the doctor said a week later, and he gave him heat treatments.

Everyone knew that Memorial Hospital was for cancer cases. Everyone but Peter Romain, his wife, Ethel, and his son, Paul. He went on the subway, but he came back in a taxi because of the collar. They said it would keep him from aggravating a possible injury in his neck. He protested, he said he could hold up his own head, but when he accepted the collar, he was harnessed to his fate.

I was visiting when he got out of the taxi. This was the first I'd heard of it, and my mother hadn't quite finished the story, so that when I saw him, the whole thing was floating loosely in my mind, ready to take any shape. It never even passed through the stage of seeming like a bad joke. The moment I saw him, I knew. I realized immediately that this pathos was beyond contradiction. He threatened to throw off the yoke, and we quickly understood our parts. "You don't really need it, but it can't do any harm." This was the kind of reasoning we were to use from then on. "You're not going, but kiss me, kiss me good-bye."

Although he was a superintendent, a full grade above a foreman, my father insisted on carrying a toolbox to every job. At the rasp of a saw, he'd pull out his tools—he would never touch theirs—and "show those monkeys how to do their job." If he saw a man choking up on the handle of a hammer, he'd snatch his own hammer out of the loop at the hip of his overalls and drive the nail home with two full-arm strokes. Now he was worried about his tools, because they were still on the job. "I don't want those monkeys fooling with my box," he said. "I better go pick it up." I tried to talk him out of it, saying that I would go and get them, but he seemed to feel that no one could conceivably move his box except under his personal supervision, so we went together.

He wouldn't wear the collar. We argued back and forth for twenty minutes, but I couldn't budge him. I was holding it out toward him as an adult holds a spoonful of medicine and tries to talk a child into swallowing it. Then, all at once, I became so intensely aware of the feel of the collar that I almost dropped it. For the first time, I perceived it as a thing. It was a sausage-shaped pad stuffed with cotton and covered with a sort of sock made of unbleached muslin. At each end the sock terminated in a string, like an apron string. It really was nothing but a simple surgical brace, but for some reason it gave me another feeling; there was something suggestively organic about it, like a fleshy deformity, voluntarily assumed.

It disgusted me, and abruptly I decided that it was not for me to take its part, so I said, "All right, if you insist," and dropped the collar on the table. Feeling that he had gained an important victory, he refused to take a taxi, too. The idea of the job made him feel himself again. He almost had me believing it.

The job was a store on the first floor of a building on West Forty-fifth Street. When we walked in, he introduced me to the carpenter foreman, whom he had talked to on the phone. The box was locked in a small storeroom to which my father still had a key. He opened the door and walked up to the box. I saw what was in his mind, so I crossed in front of him and seized it.

All my life I'd seen him with that box on his shoulder. He balanced it lightly with one hand and tipped his hat to the ladies on our block with the other. Even back when I was a child, men had stopped carrying things on their shoulders, but he did it so naturally that he never looked out of place. The box was about two and a half feet long, eighteen inches high, and six inches thick. It was made of plywood, stained mahogany, with metal-reinforced corners, and it held a surprising number of tools, because they were all ingeniously fitted into special slots. Although, as I said, I'd seen the box all my life, I'd never picked it up. I would no more have picked it up than I would have picked up my mother, as my father sometimes playfully did. Still, now that the time had come, I approached it without thinking about it.

The handle was hard. It even seemed calloused, like his hand. I bent over and wrapped my palm and fingers around it and straightened up. The tendons inside my elbow and shoulder stretched to their full length and snapped painfully taut. I almost lost my balance, and the tools clinked telltale in the box. My father looked away and glanced uncomfortably at the carpenter foreman.

In the few steps it took to reach the street, my arm was already tired. It was three blocks to the subway. He said very gently, "Put it on your shoulder, Paul," so I lifted it with both hands to my right shoulder, where it rested on a bone and cut into the muscles at the base of my neck. Although I continued to support it with both hands, I was drenched with sweat after the first block, and the muscles in my stomach were cramping on an inexplicable emptiness that seemed to have usurped the place where the seat of my strength should have been. I was more than thirty years younger, taller and heavier, and stronger, I knew, than he was, yet I felt that my blood vessels were about to burst. My legs trembling, I set my will blindly on reaching the subway. People stared at me, but I hardly noticed them, and he looked straight ahead, walking neither slowly nor fast, his face noncommittal. The expanding sensation in my loins made me forget the pain in my shoulder and in my neck. From my solar plexus to my pelvis I was ten feet long. My head was spinning, and things were whirling around me. At the end of the second block, I lurched off the curb and thought I would fall on my face, when my father's hand on my arm stiffened me and seemed to resuscitate my strength. "Wait for the light," he said.

For a blind moment I stood there, not recognizing my deliverance, then I put the box down. I felt so light then I thought I could have taken my father under one arm and the box under the other and flown home. When I picked it up again, I knew I could make it.

At my mother's incessant urging, my father agreed to wear the collar. After the first day he even wore it with a certain amount of independence, like the captain of a ship wearing a lei put around his neck by Hawaiian girls trying to sell favors to the tourists. At times he condescended to it so successfully that the *collar* seemed absurd. When we went to the hospital for his second visit, he wore it willingly, remarking that it was only to please Dr. Windelband, the chief diagnostician.

Dr. Windelband looked so much like Saint Peter that he was almost comically suited for his job. Very tall, he had iron-gray hair, bushy eyebrows, and a great decisive rudder of a nose. He greeted my father very graciously, and my father introduced him to me. I thought he shook my hand rather peculiarly, as though a handshake were a very revealing form of auscultation. I felt that he had illicitly taken some knowledge of me in that brief grip. He asked my father how he felt, and under his majestic solicitude my father naturally said fine. "That's good," he said, "because we have a little surprise on the program today. We want to get the inside story on you, so we're going to give you a cystoscopy. They can sometimes be unpleasant, but I don't think that will bother an old soldier like you."

I didn't think so either. I'd seen my father fish around in the fleshy part of his hand with a sharp knife to look for a glass splinter, and it was his boast that he had pulled one of his own teeth with a pair of pliers. After they went off down a corridor, I sat in the waiting room reading a picture story— not in a medical journal, but in a popular magazine—on "breastplasty," a new method of building up women's breasts by stuffing them with plastic sponges. I had already finished the article, and I was turning the magazine upside down to get a better look at the patient on the operating table when a nurse came out and called my name. Taken by surprise, I shut the magazine, then I looked up and she caught my eye with the curiously direct glance that only nurses seem to have, but which, this time, was softened by an expertly disciplined compassion. There was something so professional, so authoritative, about that compassion that a cold breath blew through my belly, and I jumped up out of my seat. Without a word she turned, and I followed her. In the corridor she stopped in front of a door and with a brief gesture of her hand said, "Your father is in there."

But my father wasn't in there. Sprawled on a table, incredibly out of place, lay a plaster Prometheus, middle-aged and decrepit, recently emptied by an eagle, varnished and highly glazed as though still wet. Or perhaps, when you looked closer, this was just an illusion, born of an idea, and what actually lay there was only an eviscerated old rooster, plucked white, his skin shiny with a sweat more painful than blood. . . . Whatever it was, it wasn't my father. It might have been an old man, trembling and staring into eternity, whom I helped, avoiding the puddles of his exploded bladder, to dress, and who staggered out on my arm, but he was not in the least like, bore no resemblance whatsoever to, my father, who was still a relatively young man, slim and straight, with a quick step and a dark eye.

. . .

For three days my father didn't sleep, and I didn't either. On the fourth day I presented myself at the hospital and asked for Dr. Windelband. He appeared almost immediately, wearing a white coat. Without asking me what I wanted, or why I was there, he simply walked up to me and looked at me rather speculatively, as though he were trying to guess my weight. "Come along," he said, and I followed him through the corridor to the elevator. He pressed the button and turned toward me. The elevator door opened at the same time that my mouth opened to speak, and an attendant rolled out an empty wheelchair. The doctor took my arm and drew me into the elevator. I stood beside him, facing the door, waiting for it to open on the answer. He took my arm again, and we stepped out into an empty corridor. He stopped there, looking down at me. He was so tall that he seemed to peer over every screen I might erect. "The cancer has reached his bones," he said. "I'll give him six months."

I wanted to say, "Why will you only give him six months?" but this impulse seemed to be struggling, through an immense snowdrift, to the surface, where it might take shape, so I just stood there, allowing his words to find their final location in my head without passing through the complicated machinery of recognition. They went in like a film he'd given me to develop in a darkroom, or a record to be played on my phonograph sometime when I was in a listening mood.

"Are you going to take him in as a patient?" This was all I could find to say.

He removed his pince-nez. "We don't keep incurable cases," he said.

"No, you send them packing," I said, and then I bit my lips to stop a hysterical laugh.

"There are nursing homes." He peered at an even steeper angle over the screen, so that he could see to the very bottom of me, like a man looking down a shaft. He put on the pince-nez again. "Your father's a nice man," he said, and he walked off down the corridor.

Damnation is faint praise. It's not hellfire or a Dantesque place presided over by an indefatigable devil, nor even the more sophisticated "room with other people. . . ." It's faint praise. "A nice man!" Can that phrase, or praise, penetrate an inch of eternity? Is that all sixty-two years achieve? Is that what the cystoscope said? A nice man be damned! He's a prick! He's a saint! He's a hero, a clown, a Quixote. . . .

My mother's nice husband was not doing so nicely, and it was my job to tell her. After that, someday when she was through crying, I would try to tell myself. Not now, though, there was too much else to do.

The next day, I went over. She answered the door with a faintly beseeching look in her eye, like a dog that wants to be taken for a walk. He was upstairs in bed. I felt that this was as bad a time as any. "Mom," I said, engaging her eyes for the first time in more than twenty years. "Mom," I said again, rapidly discarding words in my mind, getting no further. She looked at me as a girl looks at her first lover the first time, her eyes shiny with fear and regret and suppressed excitement, her soul splayed open to indistinguishable joy or pain, her whole being a question that strained, strained, toward an answer. . . .

"Mom," I said again, and she burst into tears on my breast, crying so copiously that after a while I felt like a child who has wet himself.

I decided to call a nursing home. I went through the Red Book and selected what seemed to be a likely place. After several rings, a woman's voice answered the phone.

"Hello," I said. "My father is a cancer patient and I would like to place him in your care."

The voice came back dry and impersonal: "Is he disfigured?"

"*Disfigured?*" I said. "I'm calling the home for cancer patients . . ."

"Yes," the voice came back without inflection, "I inquired whether the patient is disfigured. We do not accept disfigured patients."

"No! He's handsome!" I shouted. "He's beautiful!" and I disfigured her ear with the receiver.

I had a savage desire to nurse him myself, to keep our sorrow secret between us, to fight off his illness with tooth and nail, but we had to send him somewhere, because the groans were beginning to pry open his teeth. The family doctor gave him injections, but they lasted only an hour. I could tell when they wore off by the clenching of his jaws and the stare in his eyes as he locked his will around the pain and tried to contain it. The doctor came as often as he could, but after two days of this he advised me to send him to a hospital. I was seeing the doctor to the door when he paused and murmured quickly, almost furtively, "He needs more than I can give him—even if I had no other patients." This sounded more like recommending his soul to heaven than his body to a hospital, and after he had said it, observing too his own despairing tone, the doctor hesitated and swallowed, trying to swallow his remark, in obedience to the unwritten law that death shall be denied until it is certified.

"Which hospital?" I asked. "Memorial won't keep him, and as for the nursing homes—"

"Nursing homes won't do," he interrupted quickly. "He's an emergency case." He looked at me half sadly, half uneasily, afraid I might demand that he say it.

"What do I do?" I said. "Call the police emergency squad or the fire department? Isn't there someplace in this insane city where a human being can lie still and be sick? Do I have to appeal to the ASPCA?"

"You'll have to put him in Kings County," he said apologetically. "There's nothing else you can do. I'll declare him an emergency."

At that moment, by way of bidding the doctor good-bye, my father declared himself. We heard a cry that sounded as though it came from a creature that had just acquired a voice in the farthest reaches of pain, and was now exploring that pain and that voice simultaneously, intermittently confusing one with the other. I stood there like a singing teacher fascinated by a pupil who has just produced an unearthly sound, unable to decide whether this was the most beautiful sound I'd ever heard or the most bloodcurdling. The doctor ran back into the room. My mother came from the kitchen, where she had taken a habit of retreating whenever she could, but she stopped at the threshold of the door, because she was not of the initiate, and this was a matter so serious and so strange as to be a legitimate concern only for the doctor who was a professional intimate of such mysteries, and for her puzzling son, whose own mysteries must be somehow akin to this one.

Opening his bag, the doctor spoke to me over his shoulder. "Call Kings County for an ambulance," he said.

"An ambulance!" my mother said. It was true, then.

There's no use pretending that Kings County was a chamber of horrors. It wasn't—It was just a hospital with too many sick people and too few well ones to take care of them. Actually, it gave me a feeling of confidence. It impressed me as a place where everyone had gotten down to brass tacks. It was a huge factory for repairing human organisms, a factory whose commitments always exceeded its capacity, a sort of sweatshop, in fact, but one where each man did his best with whatever he had. They put in a bed for my father in a big room in a tight space which they created by shifting a dozen other beds. He fitted in like a piece in a jigsaw puzzle. There his misery had so much company that illness almost took on the aspect of a universal condition. Squeezed between the beds, their standing figures reminding me of little fences around graves, were the relatives—I felt they had to be relatives—some, their hopes already exhausted, simply looking on silently, others talking sharply, practically, daring the sick to die when there were so many chores waiting for them.

My father diverted himself by criticizing the place. He tried to discredit his illness by discrediting the hospital. He had only one good thing to say about it—the doctor in charge of his case was Jewish. Although he was a halfhearted anti-Semite, he much preferred a Jewish doctor because he believed that Jews had a better grip on life. He regarded the doctor as a sort of pawnbroker who would make his ticket pay off. He wasn't in this business for his health—or for my father's health either—but to get results.

And so we settled down to wait, my father waiting for his return to normal life, a life which he would appreciate a little more carefully thereafter, keeping out of drafts, and avoiding strains and overspiced foods, but one which he never thought of leaving; my mother waiting like an ostrich, her head buried in the sand but the rest of her offered up quivering more helplessly than ever to the inevitable catastrophe; I waiting like an actor, playing straight man to a father who was disappearing before my eyes.

There were ups and downs—the room emptied out until there were beds only along the walls with a few feet between them for us to stand in, and then there was the arrival of a new anesthetic which helped for a while—but mostly it was a process of measuring each day's ravages and denying their significance with an ever more preposterous optimism. After a week or so, he couldn't use his legs anymore, and they told me that every day he got up and fell on his face. When they gave him a wheelchair, he exhausted himself spinning through the wards and the corridors, afraid of becoming rooted to a spot. They threatened to take the chair away from him, and this so offended him—he had expected them to admire his gumption—that he only used it when absolutely necessary after that.

My mother and I relieved each other every day like sentries. She came mornings, and I arrived in the afternoon. Fifteen minutes after I'd arrive, she'd leave. It wasn't that she couldn't stay later or I couldn't come earlier—she had nothing to do, no one to cook or keep house for, and I had school only three nights a week—it was because we weren't comfortable with him together. It was harder to put on our respective acts convincingly in the presence of someone who really knew. Our acts didn't harmonize well, either. They only do in soap operas, where everyone is unanimous in a kind of homogenized grief. The extremity of the situation had thrown each of us into a crucial relation to him, and the finality of these individual equations had made them intensely selfish. When we were there together, we were artificial, ashamed of both our hypocrisy and our emotion.

Sometimes he slept while I was there, especially after a bad night. During these hours I let my vigilance sleep too, and observed the rest of the ward, seizing every detail with unconscious gratitude. My senses alerted by the close threat of impending insensibility, I saw everything in such sharp relief that I felt I had just discovered the third dimension. It was on one of those occasions that I discovered Miss Shannon, the nurse who came on duty at four in the afternoon. I'd seen her before, and I had even felt some surprise the first time, but I'd never had a chance to speculate on her. What surprised me was her astonishing freshness. She might have been one of those white-uniformed demonstrators at a department store cosmetics counter, except that she had no trace of hardness. She was the type you also see in Rheingold Beer ads, with an almost explosive smile, and so young looking that I wondered how long she could have been a nurse. Her complexion was so fair, her lips so red, her eyes so blue, that she reminded me of a patriotic image in pastels, the winner of some title such as Miss American Flag. She seemed invariably in high spirits, making her rounds with an expression of almost insane glee. I found this first surprising, then incongruous, and finally obscene. Although she fascinated me, I began to detest her, and although she seemed more candylike than carnal, I longed to bite her round, aseptic, and ungirdled behind as it moved tauntingly alive beneath her silky nylon skirt. Once, when she stood silhouetted against the window, her thighs clearly out-lined—as though by their own gleaming light—I felt for a dazzled moment a wild impulse, a kind of call, to seize her and fuck her in the middle of the floor, and thus by sympathetic magic to resuscitate those failing men to whom she must have seemed more mirage than oasis.

. . .

I didn't suffer as much as might have been expected during those weeks. Perhaps it was because I had so much time. I had time enough to think everything away. I remember reading about a man in prison who figured the square root of two to two thousand places. He proved analogically that even the confines of his tiny cell were capable of almost infinite extension. I analyzed my situation and my father's—which might also have been thought to be inescapable—into so many places that I lost sight of the problem. It was just like my efforts to write, which I usually describe in terms of an old Irish joke: A middle-aged Irish couple are visiting another shanty Irish pair. Presently, Mrs. O'Grady of the visiting couple asks where the toilet is. "There ain't any," replies her hostess. "Begorrah, thin where do ye go?" asks Mrs. O'Grady. "Why, it's as easy as pissin' out the winder," says the lady of the house. "Yis, but what of thim as has ter shit?" pursues Mrs. O'Grady. "Why, them'll shit on the floor and sweep it around until they loses it." When they didn't fly out the window, I swept my ideas around until I lost them. As a result, I came to know the cracks in the floor pretty well, but I didn't realize this until much later.

I remember one crack in particular. At the time, I had just begun some courses at the New School in order to get the veteran's allowance. One of them was a philosophy course given by a little German whose accent somehow clothed everything he said in a sort of pseudoprofundity, so that I could never separate the platitudes from the insights. On the

first night, he waited with his hands clasped on the desk and
a faint smile on his lips until we were all seated and duly
expectant. Then he shot out quickly, without any other intro-
duction, "What is the meaning of your life?" The class, of
course, laughed, and this was partly his intention, to create an
effect of startling directness—but in my condition I was like
a glass which shatters when a particular note is struck, and
this question, which I had, until then, contained, spilled all
over me. I was so carried away that I actually expected an
answer. I bent all my attention on the little German, translat-
ing each of his words into italics as it came out of his mouth.
I followed him, anticipated him, I urged him on, faster, faster!
I shifted in my seat from one digression to another, and then I
saw what was in the wind. Setting out full sail with "What is
the meaning of your life?" he circumnavigated into "What is
the meaning of meaning?" There, in that Sargasso Sea, he
becalmed me. I was both confused and bemused. I felt I had
been taken in by an elaborate and inappropriate prank, like
the people in Paris who were the victims of a notorious
Surrealist gag. They went to see a famous tragedy, advertised
with the best actors. After a portentous wait, the curtain shot
up to reveal—a tremendous rusty machine, whirring and
clanking, whistling and pumping, hissing and showering dirty
precipitated steam on starched shirtfronts and bare bosoms.
These people, though, had their indignation, and the Surreal-
ists had their joke—I, I had my father, and he, he had not only
his son but his cancer, which in spite of all the swords with
caducei on their handles still jealously guarded its secret.

I wasn't ready to give up yet. I carried my question carefully away with me, and that night it was a lullaby that put me to sleep. In the morning I had forgotten it, but when I saw my father I remembered, and then it seemed as though he must have—or be—the key to the secret. When he opened his lips to greet me, I half expected the answer—a newly coined proverb, an aphorism so apt as to seem even obvious. I looked for a radiance to rise from his flesh, I put my ear to the shell of his hollowed body as one listens to the murmur of a conch, waiting for the stage whisper. Could this pain be with a program? Can a man emaciate without meaning?

He had a thoughtful expression on his face. "You know," he said, "I haven't had an erection since September twelfth."

When I was not with my father, he usually disappeared from my mind, as I said before. I rarely reproached myself, at the time, for this; I considered it a trick of repression which he himself and my mother had taught me. It was when I came out of the elevator on his floor, when I was walking through the corridor toward his ward, that he became intensely actual again. From the door of the ward, six beds away from him, I tried to get an instantaneous estimate of his condition, I sniffed like a bloodhound for signs. There was nothing to see—he was either awake or asleep, supine in the bed, because after the first few weeks it hurt his back to sit up—but I became so accustomed to his outline under the sheets that I could tell even from the doorway when he had the bedpan underneath him. And I was always as pleased as a young mother about the bedpan, I regarded it as a good sign.

I was completely unprepared then—as though I had expected him always to remain the same—to find his hands in the air that day, immobile as death, and excruciatingly cramped in the act of sculpting a likeness of his pain. And the other astonishing thing was that no one in that ward of forty people paid any attention to those hands, which ought to have conducted the orchestrated empathy of every living soul in sight.

I ran to his bedside to find his eyes open. "What is it, Pop?" I asked. "What do you want?" His eyes seemed glazed, but at the sound of my voice they swiveled ever so slowly, traveling a great distance, until they pointed at me. I say pointed at me, but it was rather that they focused on one point immediately in front of me and one directly behind me, so that I was bracketed in a no-man's-land of his gaze. He moved his lips to speak the unspeakable, then his eyes roved away and I ran for the nurse.

She was utterly uninfected by my excitement. "My father—" I began, but she said, "All right!" rather tartly, picked up a needle wrapped in gauze, and walked alongside me to my father's bed, holding herself so aloof from my excitement that no one would have guessed that we were going to the same place for the same purpose. Unceremoniously pulling down his left arm like a vandal destroying a statue with a club, leaving the other grotesquely widowed in the air, she jabbed the needle unerringly into his vein, as you would flip a switch to turn off a motor, and put him to sleep.

I stood there looking at her, dumbfounded—whether with horror or admiration I still can't say. Then, as all the while, she wore that infernal smile, and it was at that moment that I resolved, at any cost, to wipe it off her face.

Suddenly my father became immune to anesthesia. He couldn't have chosen a better time, because his illness was at its fullest flowering, rotting his entire skelton until the very marrow of his bones ran with pain. Even the new wonder drug had hardly any effect. I became a beggar, begging the nurse for needles, for anything which would help him. She gave him as many as his constitution could stand, but they didn't make any difference. In fact, he began to hate the needle, flinching under its prick as though he wasn't already hurting to the limit of his capacity. Bizarre as it may seem, I began to believe that he was *insisting* on his pain. Just as a young mother wants to feel herself give birth, he seemed to want to feel himself go back into unbeing. Or perhaps he was trying to come to grips with his pain, to recognize the power he was wrestling with.

His struggles were not beautiful to behold, but I beheld them. I felt that it was my duty not to miss a single one of his writhings. His whole body had become a tongue, addressing its message to me. He was leaving so little behind that nothing could be ignored. I wanted to make movies of him to educate my children. Watching him, I learned that the convulsions of death and the convulsions of love differ only in that these were experienced utterly alone.

Now his strength fell away faster—and, against my will, mine grew. It seemed we had only a fixed amount to divide between us: As he gave it up, I acquired it. I tried to give it back, to refuse it, to make myself small, but the smaller I squeezed myself, expelling all my breath and deflating my chest with enormous sighs, the smaller he would shrink. We were on a seesaw, a scale, and my weight was catapulting him into oblivion.

It was too much for my mother. One morning she couldn't get out of bed to go to the hospital. The doctor came and diagnosed her illness as one that would last a little longer than my father. Now I ran from the hospital to her. We became a right-angled triangle in which I lied to her about the hypotenuse. "He's resting much better, the anesthesia works again, he asked about you, et cetera."

By that time, I was such a familiar figure around the floor that I often ate with the ward boys. When my father was asleep, I roved all over, talking to ward boys, patients, relatives. While I was on one of these jaunts, I passed Miss Shannon sitting at her desk over her reports. I thought I heard her giggle, and I turned around. This time she didn't try to smother it, she just laughed. A rage which came from somewhere else rose up in me, but a deep, urgent curiosity outweighed it, so I said, "What's so funny?" She laughed again, but my curiosity grew instead of my anger, and I said again, "What's so funny?"

"You!" she said between giggles.

"Why?" I persisted. "Why am I so funny?"

"The way you come here," she said.

"The way I come here?"

"Go on," she said, still laughing silently. "I've got my reports to make out."

Sitting beside my father's bed, I conceded that perhaps it was funny after all, the comic enigma of my devotion, and for a moment I saw myself as someone who has missed the joke, who stands by, a lugubrious and uncomprehending figure, amid general laughter. Still, I thought, true or not, it was another score to settle with her.

I saw so much more of her at that time that my obscure desire began to burn like a rash in my mind. I decided to launch a campaign, a very carefully thought-out campaign, because it had to succeed.

"You know, Miss Shannon," I said to her the next chance I got, "I think that your presence and your spirit does more for these men than the doctors' medicines."

She looked at me with mild surprise behind her smile. It was the first speech I had made her. Still, she did not seem disinclined to accept it.

"Even the doctors admit," I pursued, "that the *will* to live often means the difference between life and death. To these old men in this gray ward you are an advertisement for life. Your warm smile and your yellow hair remind them of the sun that once seemed to shine especially for them, your blue eyes just naturally suggest the sky on a perfect day, and your youth calls up a picture of a girl they knew, or married, forty years ago—or perhaps even of a grandchild today." I spoke these words with an air of wistfulness, as though I was thinking profoundly and nostalgically of my father.

Changing pace, so as not to lay it on too thick, I shifted to a different tone: "I studied philosophy in college," I said, "and I remember a professor asking us, 'What is the meaning of your life?' Well, of course, we didn't know, and neither, it turned out, did he, but I've got a notion—I can't exactly say why—that *you* know. Maybe you don't realize it, maybe you never stopped to think about it, but I think you know."

This was one of the few rare occasions when the smile left her face. When she wasn't smiling, her face seemed arrested on the brink of thought, hesitating to cross over. I leapt into the breach. "For weeks now," I said, "I've been watching you and admiring the way you carry yourself. I've wanted to talk to you, to ask you so many questions about the things you've learned, the kind of things that only intimate daily contact with life and death teaches you, the kind of feelings which a man, a doctor, wouldn't know how to receive.... But I was always afraid you'd think I was crazy if I asked you . . . or that you'd misunderstand."

I could see that this speech touched her, and at this knowledge a wave of guilt suddenly flushed through me—but it was half pang, half thrill, and it only whetted my appetite. "I know I'm keeping you from your work," I said hastily, as though interrupting myself, "I know you have no time to talk to me here . . . and so I wondered . . . well, I wondered if sometime, sometime we might talk afterward, I mean, after you leave here. . . ."

She still seemed to be trying to think, a child trying to decide whether she dared run across the street after her ball. She's really so unsophisticated, I thought. Without the needle in her hand, she was another person. She reminded me of Ray Robinson, the most stylized performer ever to climb through the ropes in Madison Square Garden, but just a simple Harlem boy outside them. Or a young ballet star, breathtaking on the stage and pedestrian in life. It was too easy, I would have to do it while she was shoving the needle in *my* arm, so that we could, like two scorpions, sting each other to death.

"Well," she said, the clouds in her eyes clearing up, "I guess so."

"Good!" I said warmly. "I'm very glad. Tonight?"

"No, tomorrow," she said, and the smile came back.

My father and I didn't talk much. We never had. When I was a child, he wouldn't; when I reached adolescence, I wouldn't. After that, we were so far apart that we couldn't have heard each other across the distance. Beyond a few fixed general remarks, he never spoke of his illness, so I didn't, either. The phrase "When I get out of here" and his use of the future tense showed that he wanted to think this way. I tried not to have to join in this, because I couldn't make it sound convincing. It's one thing for a man to choose to fool himself; as a piece of practical solipsism it has a certain reality. But when someone else chimes in, his motives being so much weaker, his contact with the lie so much less intimate and passionate, everything rings false. Besides, my presence brought him peace, and he was usually satisfied with this.

With my mother, it was just the opposite. We talked all the time, as though silence were an accusation. A thousand times, she would ask me the same questions about my father's condition, and a thousand times, I would vary the same lies. If she wanted to know, she knew. If not, well, then I'd lie like a broken record until she no longer demanded it. "I'm going to get up out of this bed and go and see him!" she would suddenly announce in a tragic voice. "No, you're not," I would answer, "I'm not going to have both of you in the hospital," and so on in that vein. We kept our mouths stuffed with platitudes so that there was no room for sudden blurts or ejaculations, for sobs or curses, truths or revelations, for admissions, recognitions, definitions, for candid remarks, apostrophes, ambiguities, aposiopeses, for embarrassing moments, slips of the tongue, for free associations, recriminations, I-told-you-so's, or for any other quirk of communication that might have created the impression that we were a mother and son aboutout to lose a husband and father.

As I came down the corridor of the hospital, my mind was teeming with schemes and scenes for my rendezvous with Miss Shannon. My heart was beating too hard, and I felt I couldn't conceal my gloating, so when I passed her desk I merely inclined my head and gave her a grave nod as if to say, We will speak later. To my surprise though, she beckoned to me, and her face was so unreadable that I thought it was all off. But she just said, "He's in there," and pointed to a doorway across from her desk, which was set in an alcove cut out of the corridor. That phrase "in there"—so nondescript, uttered so uninflectedly, accompanied by the brief gesture of a hand with a pen in it—I had heard that phrase before, and suddenly I wondered whether, in their training, they were taught such phrases to be used on painful occasions, like drugs or straitjackets. Expecting the worst, I went through the door.

Expecting the worst—that's another phrase for you. We *never* expect the worst. I didn't recognize him at first, he was so bad. His mouth was open and his breathing was hungry. They had removed his false teeth, and his cheeks were so thin that his mouth looked like a keyhole. I leaned over his bed and brought my face before his eyes. "Hello darlin'," he whispered, and he smiled. His voice, faint as it was, was full of love, and it bristled the hairs on the nape of my neck and raised gooseflesh on my forearms. I couldn't speak, so I kissed him. His cheek smelled like wax. His hand came up, light as a feather, on my shoulder. There was a chair against the wall. I pulled it up to the bed and sat down, taking his hand in both of mine. He closed his eyes. I rose out of the chair, but a vein throbbed in his neck, so I sat down again.

Sometime later—it might have been five minutes or two hours—the doctor came in. He looked at the chart at the foot of the bed, made some notes on a clipboard, and walked out. I ran after him and stopped him in the corridor to ask the inevitable question. He was young, heavyset, and competent looking, the competence crowding out all other expression from his face. He looked at me for a moment, and said, "A day, two days. . . ."

I went in and sat down again, taking his hand again in mine. His eyes were closed. "A day, two days. . . ." Here it was. All at once, the reality of it yawned in my mind and found me standing on a brink, like an Arctic explorer looking out alone over endless fields of ice. I would have liked to cry—a great loop curled through my being—but I could not. I could not cry for my father, and *this* realization brought the tears to my eyes.

My proposed encounter with Miss Shannon seemed more incongruous than ever, but I had had enough of congruousness. I let her know I would wait, and she accepted this with her standard smile. I went out to the candy store across the street and bought a book. Then I settled down beside my father, who was asleep, and waited for one thing or the other.

I had selected a paperback Western. I learned to read them in the army, like Eisenhower. The hero was the usual superman, but instead of being grim-jawed or tight-lipped, he had a sense of humor. His name was Happy Jack or something like that, and he had a homely Will Rogers kind of philosophy. Toward the middle of the book he got off a remark that wrenched me suddenly back to reality. In a crisis, everything wrenches you back to reality. He said, "I want to have so much fun that when I die I'll laugh like hell."

I was making the obvious comparison this remark suggested when they wheeled another bed into the room. The room was long and narrow, so they situated it below the foot of my father's bed. Lost in the sheets and pillow, I saw a dark spot, apparently a Negro patient to keep my father company in death's antechamber here outside the ward, like the exit chamber in a submarine from which you ascend to the surface through ever-decreasing pressures. The man was so thin that his form was wholly invisible under the sheets, even on this hard bed. As soon as the bed was in place, the doctor wheeled in a plasma rack, hung the plasma bottle, and inserted the tube in the dying man's arm. A woman stopped the doctor outside the door, a little spare woman, very dark and angular. She was dressed neatly, but twenty years out of date, and she wore her hat pulled down and straight across her brow. She too asked the question; then, walking resolutely up to the bed, she looked down at the sick man the way a workman approaches his bench. "Lord!" she exclaimed, "Lord! Come down and help this man! Come down and help your child! This is your child you redeemed with your blood, Lord!" She had a strong West Indian accent, which gave her speech a precise, ceremonious quality. "Lord!" she cried again, her right hand seizing the plasma rack, whose short horizontal bar formed a cross, "Lord! Come down and *take* your child! Come down and *carry* him to glory!" The plasma bottle with its translucent tube undulating El Greco-like beneath was a hydrocephalic Jesus on that cross. "Lord!" she exclaimed again, "I'm praying to you, Lord! I'm praying to you to *take* your child into everlasting immortality!"

I had stopped listening to her. I was thinking, to whom can I recommend my father? To the mortician? Where is his

everlasting immortality? In the city records? Why isn't he one
of God's children? Because he's a nice man instead? As midnight approached, I felt like a time bomb. I kept expecting her
to break it off. But at twelve o'clock she was ready, with a
trench coat over her white uniform. "Where do you live?" I
asked, praying for the right answer. "West Seventy-sixth
Street," she said, and it was as I had hoped, in the same
direction as my place.

On the subway I plied her with talk to get her off guard,
philosophical talk to establish an atmosphere of shared irre-
futability. I put the conversation on the level of values, I
conjured up a fog of confused sincerity, the kind of sincerity
that is behind most of the drastic, dispassionate mistakes girls
make. She followed willingly enough, but very passively, as
though she were tired and wanted to be carried. As the doors
were opening on the Fourteenth Street station, I seized her
and pulled her out of the train, exclaiming in a confidential
voice, "I know a wonderful little place where we can talk
in peace!"

I led her to the most deserted bar I could think of, and
we took a booth in the corner. She consented to a double
bourbon. I couldn't decide whether to keep leading her—it
was the safer way—or to draw her out, because I wanted more
of her included. But she wouldn't be drawn out, even with the
bourbon. She just smiled and nodded and answered briefly.
The smile, I noticed with some surprise, had changed. It had
changed from a meaningless, artificial explosion to an almost
rueful expression with a hint of complicity behind it. I judged

that it was about time. "Listen," I said, borrowing a tone of urgency from another source, "I want to give you a book. A book that was written for you, a book that belongs to you as much as your diary, that's dedicated to you like your nurse's certificate."

I called for the check, paid it quickly, and led her out by the arm. My apartment was four blocks away, so I bridged the distance with talk, raving about *Journey to the End of the Night,* the book she needed like she needed a hole in her head. She followed me without the slightest hesitation, but so passively that she made me think of a blind person being escorted across the street.

Going up the four flights, my eyes were so intent on the pink beneath her white stockings—I thought I even discerned delicate blue veins—that I stumbled and had to steady myself by seizing the banister. I had cleaned and ordered the apartment with an obsessive devotion, and I snapped on the lamp expecting her exclamation, but she said nothing, she just walked three steps further into the room and stopped. "Take off your coat," I said, and she unbuttoned it for me to remove. I strode over to the bookshelf, still following the script, and seized the Céline. When I turned with it in my hand, about to hold it out, I saw the futility of the gesture in her eyes. Confused, but undismayed, I let the book fall and seized her in a death grip and bore her backward to the bed, where I took her with all her clothes on. Working with feverish haste, I nailed the coffin, dug the grave, and dropped my precious load.

Sometime later I woke and impatiently pulled her clothes off under the bright light, exposing her pastel body like a calendar painting in its inhuman healthiness. Taking up my task again, I bore the pall, trod the tread of the dead, bowed my head, and tamped down the ruffled earth. I put all my strength into pounding it, pounding it flat, but it remained stubbornly round, heaving against me. I tried, I tried, but flowers sprang up under the blade of my shovel, and I dropped it.

I was in a hospital, in bed, and a nurse was standing over me, smiling. Where was the needle in her hand? I wondered, and then, as my head began to clear, she spoke. But I couldn't make out what she said, and before I could answer she was gone.

My father broke down at last, and fear haunted his eyes for the first time. When I came in, he gave me a drowning look which told me plainly that he had been adrift in uncharted seas. His eyes sucked me in. They were twin drains in a sink down which blackish waters swiftly disappeared, suddenly widening as the tides ran out. They nursed, like infant mouths, on me. I tried to find some formula to feed them, but I felt shamefully inorganic. "Don't leave me alone," he whispered, "I'm afraid." I put my hand on his. "You're not alone, Pop," I said, "I'm here." His eyes went far away. "I wish I had a hundred of my children here, and their children," he said, "I don't want to be alone." You're not alone, Pop," I said again, "I'm with you." "Yeah, I know, honey," he said, "I know," but there was no sense of solace in his tone, and I knew what he felt. You want everybody on earth to stop what they're doing and come to say good-bye *personally* to you. You want *humanity* to see you off, the way close friends see you off on a boat. The idea of unanimity, two billion people's sympathy, is the only commensurate condolence. I did my best. I tried to refuel him with filial devotion, to plug him into some unequivocal center or source, some socially recognized certainty, by virtue of which he could say, "Therefore I am," and through which he could feel himself perpetuated. . . . I tried to radiate sonlight, to show him his way and warm him on his journey . . . but I concentrated myself so hard, so crystalline, willed myself so clearly, that I could only twinkle like a diamond. I turned my straining eyes on him like magnifying glasses with no son behind them. I tried, I tried, but the more I strained, the less was I able to make our relatedness *immediate,* the more I saw him, and made him see me—I can't say it any other way—*sub specie aeternitatis.*

The Lord had come down to take his child, so we were alone in the white oblong room, like an equation written on a piece of paper. At that moment, the imminence of emptiness was so immense that everything was reduced to a mathematical perspective, to an anxiety to introduce order into that void, to pull it into finiteness by a far-flung grapple of my will.

Miss Shannon was outside at her desk, and I knew that something lay between us, I felt some needle in me trembling on that point. Something lay between us, it was a carpet rolled out for me to walk on, but I could not, my mind was still struggling like a monkey wrench to squeeze an inconceivable space down to some possible size. Space had suddenly become tragedy to me, and I needed all my will to look out on it. Miss Shannon was millions of light years away, farther away than a star. Falling like a comet, I had passed near her, felt the pull of her gravity, but now I had plunged beyond.

The following day he fell into a coma. When I came in and looked into his face, I found no sign of recognition. His eyes stared out unfocused, like a newborn child's. I tried to engage them with my own, I tried like a hypnotist to synchronize them with my will, but they would not. I stared into them until I had to come up for air, and then on their surface I saw myself bloated almost beyond recognition, a corpse risen from their depths. His gaze cast back into his mind, far-flung, flung out of focus into an infinite space, not simply folding back on itself but fixed on some point in inner space, as a navigator charts his course on a star, or a man with a word on the tip of his tongue casts his eyes back through the dictionary of his experience, seeking that word in a void of silence. "Pop," I said softly, letting my voice sink gently into the pool of his eye like a line, "Pop," but there was no ripple to undulate centrifugally worldward, no stir in that Coney Island mirror which had once immortalized, and now monstered, my image.

The doctor was standing beside me, his ever-present clipboard in his hands. All at once with that clipboard he reminded me of a dispatcher at an airport. I looked him squarely in the face, studying him carefully for evidence of contradiction, as though he were about to lie. He looked squarely back at me, and between us passed a tacit understanding, as in the movies one spy slips forbidden information to another. "Can he hear me?" I asked. "Yes," he said, his expression becoming competent again, impersonal, until he might have been discussing a theory of poetry, "Yes, he can hear you, but he can't answer."

Again I crouched over my father as the doctor went out. He can hear me, but he cannot answer; this coma, then, would be his coda. I stood there gathering the threads together, and as I looked down that long street I had a strong sense of déjà vu. I was in Pennsylvania Station, in uniform. It was my final leave before going over, and at that stage the odds were not in our favor. He knew it, and insisted on taking me to the train. We were standing in the aisle, facing each other, when the conductor sang out "All aboard!" as if he were some omnipotent arbiter dividing us into two groups destined for different fates. This cry froze us in our farewell, so that we were caught there, frozen in an instant of recognition, eternalized in a classical moment which turned us into statues kinetic with a terrific frozen impulse. Finally he put out his hand, and I gripped it with a vague force. He put his other hand on my shoulder, and now we were a modern tableau, all our tragic poise gone. "Keep punching, boy," he said, and the moment died. He disappeared down the aisle, and from my throat. I stared idly out the window, the moment thrown away like a cigarette at the entrance to a movie. I waited for the platform to move, but suddenly he was out there on it, a performer, unapplauded, ineptly come back for an encore. His lips moved, he was saying something to me. I couldn't hear through the double pane, so I nodded and smiled. He spoke again. I said aloud, "That's right, Pop," and people turned and looked at me. The train didn't move. He was going to wait. He unbuttoned his coat and, seizing the lapel, swung it open as you would a door, at the same time bending his head sharply sidewise until he seemed to be smelling his armpit. This elaborate pantomime explained that he was drawing a cigar from his pocket. He held it up for me to see. "See, I'm going to smoke a cigar while I wait for the train." "Yes, I see, you're going to smoke a cigar while you wait for the train." He struck a match and cupped it unnecessarily in the breezeless station. Hunched over his cupped palms, he puffed powerfully and rhythmically, like a locomotive slowly starting. It didn't start. Tilting his head back, he withdrew the cigar from his mouth, holding it at arm's length and exhaling a cloud of smoke. The train didn't move. He spoke to me again. I nodded and smiled, but something came over his face, some urgency which he had been inducing all this while like a constipated person reading a newspaper on the toilet. He began to gesticulate and move his jaws grotesquely, shaping words which before would not be molded by his mouth. The train began to move in slow spasms. He walked alongside, gesticulating and grimacing. I rose out of my seat, semaphoring through the glass. Now he was running. . . .

I took up where we had left off. "Pop," I said, "you've been a good father, just what I wanted, just what you were supposed to be. You made me into a good son, and I'll always remember. You did what you were supposed to do, you don't have to reproach yourself with anything. I'm proud of you, and you can be proud of yourself, too. I love you, Pop, just like a son loves his father, and as a man, too. God bless you, Pop."

I talked to him like this for a long time, crouched close, not because I cared whether anyone else heard, but because I wanted him to hear. As I spoke, listening to my own words as though they were the judgment of some third party, I realized with a mild astonishment that they were true.

Suddenly his eyes rolled in a wild surmise. I started, and almost lost my balance, as though I were standing on those wildly rolling orbs. What had he seen, where had his spirit careened? What was it that passed through him and spun his eyes like the spinning wheels of an overturned car?

"Pop," I said, bending nearer, "Pop," but as I opened my lips to let out this vowel, he gave a huge sigh and shot a great breath into my mouth. I caught it full, and it went all through me. I swallowed it like a toast, not knowing whether it was poison or elixir. I swallowed it full, and it inflated me until I swelled incredibly in the mirror of his eyes.

It was minutes before I realized that his heaving chest had gone quiet. Frantic, my eyes sought the vein in his neck. "Nurse!" I called, "Nurse!"

She bent over him, looked into his eyes and saw my image there, and drew the sheet over his face. For the second time, that great loop curled through me, trying to unfurl me, to shake out my length, untie my knot. I ran through the corridor to the stair. Halfway down, I folded, crouched on a step with my fists on my temples. I wanted it to come, I thrust my hand down the throat of my grab-bag being, but drew nothing out. It was like trying to start a cold motor. The last time had been in anger, eighteen years ago, at him. . . .

They wheeled him out of the land of the living, leaving only a small plastic bag in which his glasses and his false teeth rattled. Miss Shannon had it on her desk. I held it in my hand as she held me in her eyes. We stood there, the way my father and I stood in the train. "If—" I said, and then I stopped, because I knew that the next word would be "only." She smiled the way she had that morning, and that was all we could do.

The ward boys looked very carefully at me as I walked down the corridor for the last time, studying my face for the reflection of death refracted through the living, but I had nothing new to show them, not yet.

Outside, the ground was covered with ice and the wind bit at my hands, but I welcomed it. I looked at the high gates and felt like a man released from prison. Passing the psychiatric ward, I saw a gray-clad figure, staring out of a heavily screened window with a wistfulness that only a maniac could feel. Watching him, I slipped on a little icy incline. My feet slid suddenly forward and I was about to fall when, without my willing it, my right foot shot backward to brace me, and I poised there a second, one foot in front of the other, arms extended for balance like a tightrope walker, then I recovered myself. All at once I felt exhilarated. How alive I was, how quick. . . .

"The king is dead. Long live the king!" I said to my mother. She spoke the language of hysteria, which I have never learned, but which I suspect is made up of clichés. I looked over her shoulder while she wet my shirt again. What if it were she? I thought. He died drily, after all, withering like a rose pressed in a book. He is the romance, but isn't she the reality? How organic she is, how unabstract. She could not wither or crumble—she could only putrefy, or melt, like the snails I poured salt on in our backyard. That must not happen, I knew, and then and there I placed her in the refrigerator of my heart.

I decided on the least expensive funeral. He hadn't left much insurance, and the house in the country had taken most of the money in the bank. I went to one of the big funeral chains, one which always stressed "correctness" in its ads. The entire front of the place—which they called a "chapel" although it was designed like a store—was of glass, so that the reception room where I announced the death of my father was an enormous show window. The clerk who received me referred to my father as "the deceased," which jarred on my nerves each time. I would have preferred hearing him called by his name, or referred to as my father. That's who he was, not "the deceased." If that would have sounded as though we were burying him alive, why that was all right too, because it was nearer to the truth.

Paying no attention to his niceties—he looked at me very gingerly, as if I were an important personage whose fly was open in public—I questioned the clerk about prices and finally said that I wanted a funeral as inexpensive as was consonant with simple dignity. This last phrase put him on his feet again, and we agreed on a price, which he described as a "ceremony."

Two days later I went back to "complete the arrangements." I had no idea what this meant, but I went. I was received by another clerk, and I identified myself, after which he said, "Would you like to see your father?" He said it just as a private secretary would, and suddenly I felt, Who were all these people intermediating between my father and me? I should have taken a shovel and buried him myself.

I allowed myself to be led into a room. I waited for the clerk to make that gesture of the nurses, but his arms seemed to be sewed to his sides. He made a slight bow and disappeared. Standing just inside the door, I looked at the deep box, painted slate gray, its cover propped open like a jewel case to reveal a satin lining. I walked up to it, and then I saw a sight for which I will hold my fellow citizens responsible to my dying day, a sight for which I will forgive them only when I have made each one see himself in that same light. They had painted my father like a picture postcard, and padded his cheeks the way they pad their shoulders and brassieres. They had produced his death in Technicolor, with 3-D, and painted a happy ending on him the way an old whore paints her face.

· · ·

I decided to have him cremated. His ashes would be closer to his essence than the thing in the coffin. Besides, I didn't want to tie his memory to a little oblong of bought ground where he would rot with thousands of strangers. I was to be the only one at the funeral. My mother was still in bed, and I had discouraged all the family friends. This was between him and me, and besides, I knew that they would feel obliged to discuss the cheapness of the coffin among themselves.

I presented myself for the third time at the "chapel," and I was led out the back door where they sneaked out the bodies. I sat next to the hearse driver, and we set out for the cemetery. Halfway there, I was struck by the obscurity, the loneliness, the lack of reciprocal stir, of visible displacement, that attended my father's death. At first, I felt inclined to take the blame, but I knew it was his own fault, so I compromised and resolved to make up—I didn't know how, but I'd make up—for it.

Most of the way we drove through ordinary streets, but for the last few miles we were on a highway. For some reason the highway seemed more appropriate to our procession, if you can call a one-vehicle funeral a procession. The streets made me feel that we were in a delivery truck or a taxi. Finally we entered the cemetery and arrived at a stone building. The driver led me into what I suppose they would have called another chapel. It had several small pews, and up in front where the altar would normally be was a single pew, facing the wall at a distance of perhaps a yard. A faded velvet curtain or drape covered the wall directly in front of this pew.

A big man who looked exactly like a plainclothesman in the movies came in. "Do you wish a service said?" he asked me. I said no and with that he ushered me to the single pew facing the drape. Not understanding anything here, but feeling resigned, I sat down. A few seconds later I jumped up again when a muffled and discordant hurdy-gurdy struck up behind me. I spun around—the plainclothesman was seated at what seemed to be a toy organ, playing an ungainly hymn by ear. I couldn't take it in, what he was up to, and he had me hypnotized until I heard the curtain sliding. Turning toward the wall again, I was sure then that I was in some askew wonderland such as I've traveled in dreams. The parted velvet uncovered a plate-glass window, through which I could see, a few yards away, a little elevated track about waist-high. Out of nowhere, slowly moving along the track by magic, my father's coffin appeared, floating along like a little trolley car, painted gray like the old maintenance type which carried not passengers but workmen. I stared at it as I would have stared at a floating ghost performing a feat of levitation. Suddenly at the end of the track, in what appeared to be a solid wall, a door yawned open, and I found myself looking into an inferno. The organ, the window, the track, the inferno, the plainclothesman . . . I had lost my balance and I was as close as I'll ever come to screaming when my father disappeared into the flames.

In the dim hallway, I made out a box before my door, a square box, maybe a foot deep. I was pleasantly surprised, and mentally observed that I was not expecting a package. My birthday was nowhere near, nor any holiday, and I hadn't ordered anything. For a moment I was angry at the deliverer for his carelessness in leaving it there where anyone might steal it. I picked it up, noticing with satisfaction its solid weight, but then even in the dimness I made out the cemetery's name.

Here we were again. Another encounter in our endless series. I was actually glad to see him. I remembered then that I had refused to put him in that dovecote which was lined with loving cups commemorating games lost and races run. I took the box inside, and without opening it I placed it on the bookshelf.

I'd heard that ashes were supposed to be scattered from a hilltop to the four winds, or poured into the headwaters of a river going out to sea, but as I looked at the box on the shelf, I knew that those were not our ways. We knew each other much too well for that kind of make-believe. My mind was working with an unprecedented sureness, and without going into all the details, it gave me to understand one thing very clearly. It was my job to sift those ashes, and sift them I would, until he rose from them like a phoenix.

EPILOGUE

Anatole's father died in 1948. Twelve years later I met him on the platform of the IRT waiting for a train. My father and my mother, too, had died a few years before; perhaps our common experience of death was part of what drew us together. Although we never talked about these things, as I look back it seems that there must have been something that each of us saw in the other—that we had both been in the land of the dying. For being in the presence of death is like being in a foreign land, and its geography gave shading and resonance to the rest of Anatole's life.

Anatole lived with his cancer for fourteen months. He was diagnosed in August 1989 and died in October 1990. In the early months of his illness there was reason for optimism. Both statistics and doctors hinted that "the neighborhood of years" might be a decade.

Anatole was followed by a team of doctors from the Dana Farber Institute and the Brigham and Women's Hospital in Boston. Through March 1990 the treatment, which consisted of hormonal injections and oral medications, kept the cancer in check, but in early April the disease began to break through. At this point, optimistic and in good spirits, Anatole looked and felt quite well. It was difficult to believe that the cancer was spreading. In May we went to France for ten days, traveling with friends through the Dordogne. There was adventure, much laughter, and extraordinary food, but the monthly counts indicating the spread of cancer continued to rise.

The pain of the illness began in the middle of June. Anatole needed heavy doses of codeine and analgesics. Despite the side effects of nausea and drowsiness, he managed to juggle the pain and medications in a way that allowed him to keep writing his weekly column for The New York Times Book Review. *There had been plans to begin radiation therapy, which can lessen pain, but Anatole chose instead to try an alternative treatment of diet and enzymes for a few months, hoping that this could reverse the cancer.*

He struggled and he succeeded in maintaining his sense of self, being ironical and graceful as the disease shrank his body and robbed him of his health and well-being. He wrote in his journal, "With the tubes and the weight loss, I have to recapture myself and my beauty. I have to reinvent myself."

For Anatole, style was a critical issue in his life. Being a literary critic was a way for him to speak about style, about form, and about presence. Style was for Anatole a bid for immortality, his defense against the darkness. He also saw it as society's defense against chaos and formlessness. A close friend, Michael Vincent Miller, says, "For Anatole style was a means of connecting with eternity, and literature a replacement for religion, a way to cope with death."

At the end of August there were more complications of the disease, which could only be attended to in a hospital. On August 28 Anatole was admitted to the Brigham and Women's Hospital. A week later he was transferred to the Dana Farber Cancer Institute across the street. Five weeks later he died.

Anatole's long love affair with books and writing had served him well. As a child he had wanted to become a writer. It gave him the reference points, coordinates, metaphors, and attitudes that enabled him to be alive and himself until that was no longer possible. When he lost the ability to speak, his smile was still radiant.

Anatole died doing what he did best, commenting on life and his surroundings. And yes, he was alive, as he had hoped, when he died.

ALEXANDRA BROYARD

JULY 16, 1991

CHILMARK, MASSACHUSETTS

A NOTE ON THE TYPE

This book was set in a digitized version of Garamond, a typeface originally designed by the famous Parisian type cutter Claude Garamond (1480–1561). This version of Garamond was modeled on a 1592 specimen sheet from the Egenolff-Berner foundry, which was produced from types thought to have been brought to Frankfurt by Jacques Sabon.

Claude Garamond is one of the most famous type designers in printing history. His distinguished romans and italics first appeared in Opera Ciceronis *in 1543–44. While delightfully unconventional in design, the Garamond types are clear and open, yet maintain an elegance and precision of line that mark them as French.*

Composed by ComCom, Allentown, Pennsylvania.
Printed and bound by Haddon Craftsmen, Inc.,
Scranton, Pennsylvania
Designed by Iris Weinstein